THE GRIEF ROAD MAP

FINDING YOUR ROAD AND LIFE AFTER LOSS

BY BRUCE LEISY

Published by Grief Road Map Publishing
Printed in the United States of America
ISBN 978-0-578-61414-4
Illustrations by Matt Leisy

Contents

Preface

If you inherit land, you must farm it, if you inherit a story, you must tell it.

—Swahili proverb

I am a hospice "first responder." It has been my privilege to *respond* to the death call in the home for hundreds of our hospice patients to help families navigate their grief. I am a grief counselor with a hospice agency in a large health system in Kansas City. My charge is to provide grief and emotional support to patients and families in their homes and at our hospice house from diagnosis to the end of life and beyond. The first response is often just the beginning of my work. After a patient's death, I am honored to follow bereaved family members for as long as they need my support after their loss.

This book is inspired from what our patients and their grieving loved ones have taught me. The wisdom of the following pages is gleaned from the daily interaction I have with grievers. My work with those who have suffered loss is my research. The following pages have been developed and expanded from the curriculum I wrote for the *Beyond Grief: What's Next?* workshops I lead. These workshops were suggested by two bereaved men who wanted a group focused on the future, a *road map* for their future after loss. I have *road tested* the ideas and concepts presented in this book through numerous face-to-face meetings, bereavement phone calls, emails, support groups, and workshops.

This book is the story I have inherited that I must tell to help others who are struggling with loss. I am in awe of the courageous steps taken by those who grieve. To pick up the broken pieces of their hearts and lives, and begin the arduous journey of healing after loss can be daunting. I am privileged to witness firsthand such beautiful growth and transformation of those who grieve over time. I owe a debt of gratitude to the men, women, and children from whom I learn every day and who have inspired me to write this resource for those suffering from loss, grief, and bereavement. I also am indebted to my colleagues at Saint Luke's Home Care and Hospice whose selfless dedication to our patients and families inspire me daily.

I wear a rubber bracelet on my wrist inscribed with the words: *Thankful for Life* and my daughter's name *Rachael*. At age twenty, Rachael was diagnosed with a rare blood cancer and given a 38 percent chance of living. Fortunately, she survived a very difficult chemo regimen and bone marrow transplant. During her cancer journey, "Thankful for Life" became our family motto with a double meaning. For me, wearing this bracelet is a daily reminder to give thanks for the gift of life from Rachael's bone marrow donor, Mike, and her wonderful medical team. It also serves as a keen reminder to be thankful each day for the gift of being alive in this beautiful but often challenging world.

I was humbled by the support our family received at this challenging time. For our family, we were motivated to give back to support families struggling with the impact of loss. At the suggestion of a physician friend of mine, I began a career in hospice, specializing in grief, loss, and bereavement counseling. My wife, Llinos, joins me in her work at our Hospice House supporting patients and families as a volunteer and community events coordinator. For our family, we have come full circle—we have arrived home.

Introduction

There is a time for departure even when there's no certain place to go.

—Tennessee Williams, "Camino Real"

To know the universe itself as a road, as many roads, as roads for traveling souls.

—Walt Whitman, "Song of the Open Road"

Grief, we often hear, has no *road map* or *destination*. The premise of this book is the opposite. Not only do each of us have our own unique destination in grief, we also have the ability to design a personalized *road map* to help get us there. Your destination is the journey to healing, to know and experience joy and happiness again as you begin to shape your new identity without your loved one. If you are reading this, you no doubt have experienced a significant loss in your life. This is a book of *lost and found* and I am confident that this book, armed with your direct involvement, will help you find your lost self after loss.

Purpose

The purpose of this book is to guide you to your destination—your *new* personal life direction after loss—by helping you create *Your Road Map to the Future*. By combining inward reflection and outward action, and working at your own pace, it is my great desire that this book will shine a light on your road ahead, and to give you HOPE that your journey and destination after loss can be both purposeful and beautiful. This is about you and for you. This book is designed for those who have lost their go-to person and now are learning to navigate life on their own. It is about helping you answer the question, "What's next?" after your challenging loss. Your loss may be a spouse, partner, soul mate, or significant other. Maybe you lost a parent, sibling, close friend, or child, or you may be experiencing multiple losses of loved ones. Loss does not discriminate. Now is the time, without your loved one by your side as an encourager or sounding board, to invest both in yourself and your future. It will be well worth the effort.

Have you ever driven in another country? On a different side of the road? Have you tried to understand traffic signs in other nations? Grief is a "foreign" land and as a griever you may experience the baffling world of loss. It would be my privilege to walk alongside you to serve as your guide, perhaps driver's ed instructor, to help you on the road to that elusive but expectant land ahead, known as Beyond Grief.

Getting Your Steering Wheel Back

This book carries with it both the *promise* and *challenge* of change. You have already been deeply affected by change and perhaps without much warning. One man told me after he lost his wife of over fifty years of marriage, "I feel like I lost my steering wheel."

I was captivated by the imagery of a steering wheel as this gentleman recounted the following story from his childhood in North Carolina: "I remember my grandfather saying when he came in from the fields after a day of farming soon after losing his wife, 'I feel like I lost my steering wheel.'" He stated that these same words were again repeated by his father upon the loss of his wife and, finally, now himself. Three generations of men losing their wives, and their steering wheels. All three reportedly had said, "I didn't really know what this meant until it happened to me." And with your loss, you now know as well. With your careful reading and working through the exercises in this book, it is my sincere hope you will be able to right the course you are on and get your steering wheel back.

What to Expect from This Book

This book has application for all loss. We grieve—must grieve—all losses. A death changes everything, compounding losses, such as the loss of cook, loss of social networker, loss of handyman, or loss of that second income. Non-death losses— the end of a relationship, a divorce, or job loss—can be devastating as such losses often carry with them the extra weight of rejection, shame, or dysfunction, and economic consequences. In the pages ahead, the lessons and assignments can be applied to non-death losses as well. There is no judging or comparing of losses, as the only focus is the burden that *you* carry as a result of the loss.

This book meets you where you are. You may be three weeks out after your loss, or three months, or even three years. If you are stuck, struggling, or sinking from your loss, I invite you to put the ideas and suggestions in the following pages into action that makes sense for you.

More than half of the challenge and difficulty of grief is feeling that . . .

- You are worthy.

- You are allowed to move forward.

- You even want to move forward.

The lesser challenge is making it happen.

Can I expect immediate help with my grief? Yes, you will feel immediate relief that there is a plan, a road map that is uniquely yours, ready for you to design and implement. You will also understand that the long-term benefits of this book take time and application which will require you to be realistic and patient in the days ahead. I have confidence through my work with those who have suffered great loss, that you have the raw materials, the underpinnings to make this a successful journey. No, I will not promise all smooth roads ahead, because you may face road delays or detours, but I will promise progress as you process your loss and move forward.

How to Use This Book

Start with a bird's-eye view of the road ahead. Skim through this book first to orient yourself with the layout and general concepts presented in the chapters ahead. It is written in vignette style, with short sections and spot illustrations to serve as mile markers. You are encouraged to personalize this book by writing notes in the margins, these can be comments or questions that will be of future use to you. There will be opportunities to reflect and write your responses to questions and exercises. Over time you may want to reread a section, as its importance and relevance becomes more evident to you over the passage of time. This book has four parts:

Part 1: YOUR DESTINATION AWAITS—The Road Ahead. Begin by reading the opening section on your destination, this is where you are headed. This section examines where you are, where you are going, and why to make the decision to move forward. Next is your road map planning and preparation, your foundation for your life ahead.

Part 2: DOING—The Main Road. This section focuses on your outward actions. Suggestions and assignments are designed to help you move forward to healing, feeling both alive and normal again.

Part 3: BEING—The Inner Road. This section focuses on your emotional and inner well-being.

Part 4: DETOURS, GROWTH, AND DESTINATION—The Hard and Beautiful Road. This section begins with the inevitable detours and stretches of rough road you may encounter. It concludes with a focus on your personal growth, legacy, and destination through and beyond grief.

Highlighted Features

Be on the lookout for the following:

Truths from the Road: Be sure to visit these important sections throughout the book that highlight what grievers have told me on important topics on their road to healing. There is comfort and wisdom in what others who "have been there" have to say. We learn from one another. *Why not circle any that apply to you? Or write a response in your notebook to, "What would you say?"*

Quotes from Notable Persons: Expect to see quotes from notable authors at the beginning of sections. *Why not write a quote that speaks to you on a note card and place in a visible position in your home or car to help guide you on this journey?*

"Road" Scholar Assignments: Be sure to complete the suggested, but optional exercises and assignments in the Road Scholar sections throughout this book. Putting time into these exercises will help you on your road to renewal.

Blank Road Signs: Look out for blank road signs at various spots throughout this book. Post what is on your mind at the time: your progress, speed, or other observations. You decide.

Other Roadside Attractions: Milepost Tips, Scenic Overlooks, Epiphany Alerts

Expect to encounter your emotions. Embrace traveling through tough neighborhoods on your way to your destination home. Tears, smiles, and laughter are in your travel forecast.

Expect to be overwhelmed. Put this book down if you feel overwhelmed. This is normal. Pick it up when you are ready. Go at your own pace. There is no reward for speed.

This book is your companion. For the year ahead and beyond, keep this book nearby as a reference, and for future tune-ups. Think of it as your trusted road atlas, well-worn from trips, or a map that has been folded and refolded many times and is thin along the crease.

What You Will Need for This Journey

You will need a notepad and a calendar to complete the exercises and assignments in this book. I recommend that you keep a separate What's Next? notebook for all your thoughts and plans. You will need an open mind and you should carry a sense of expectation. You should look forward to soaking up an extra helping of *hope and inspiration* as well as *trust and aspiration* as you read. My title for our time together is Encourager-in-Chief. I applaud your courage to embark on this journey, this great adventure, and I thank you for joining me on this road, your ROAD TRIP through and beyond grief to your *new you*.

Part 1
YOUR DESTINATION AWAITS—The Road Ahead

Welcome to Your Destination

One's destination is never a place, but a new way of looking at things.
— Henry Miller, *Big Sur and the Oranges of Hieronymous Bosch*

Country roads, take me home / To the place I belong . . .
— Bill Danoff, John Denver, Taffy Nivert Danoff, "Take Me Home, Country Roads"

THE GREAT REVEAL:
(Warning: Spoiler Alert)

Your Road Map Beyond Grief Destination Is . . .

HOME

Home is your destination. Home is not a physical place or location, but what we carry within ourselves. To be home, at home in our own skin. This is where we are headed together. Arriving home again is to be at peace with yourself, expecting to discover a whole world about yourself as you become "whole" again. *Looking forward to welcoming you HOME.*

Your destination is → to LIVE again.

Your destination is → to feel NORMAL again.

Your destination is → to become WHOLE again.

Your destination is → to arrive HOME again.

Your destination is to feel normal again. No secret, no surprise, this is where we are headed, and we will soon be on the road to get there. Chances are that whatever you are feeling today, that it is perfectly normal and natural for the loss you have suffered. This is simply part of the grieving process. People who are grieving tell me, "I just want to feel normal" or "I want to feel the way I used to feel" or "I want to get my joy back." One woman told me after sixty-four years of marriage, that she is "doing OK but I'm still looking for my 'new normal' that friends tell me about." Clearly, we understand that we cannot turn the clock back to what was our previous normal before loss, and we also know deep inside that we want life to take on a feeling of normalcy again. So, with that in mind, your road map is designed to help you get there.

Your destination is arriving at that wide spot in the road, when you can begin to feel joy again, begin to see some meaning and purpose in your life, to have a sense of gratitude and a reason to get up in the morning. You will know that you are healing when your loss is not the very first thing you think of when you wake up in the morning. That punch to the gut. Simply put, your destination is *to live again*. This is your Road Map Destination. Let's work together to find out how you can reach this destination which seems so distant.

This Is a Destination Book

With this book, you have tools to design your road map to your new destination. Above is what your destination will look like, with plenty of opportunity for you to put your finishing touches on your new destination home. This is your placeholder, so you know where you are headed. Just like a "destination wedding" this is a "destination book," this is where I hope you as a griever are headed. Your destination is fueled by hope, by trust, and by doing and being. Welcome aboard, your destination may take time, but the healing will be in the journey.

All Roads Lead to Your Destination

The roads of peace, joy, purpose, renewal, and transformation all lead to your Destination Home, your *new you*. Your destination is fueled by hope and trust and by DOING and BEING.

Your Destination Home Mileposts

Peace—To live again

Joy—To feel normal again

Purpose—To feel whole again

Renewal—To feel the power of healing

Transformation—To arrive home again

Begin with Your Destination in Mind

Your road map begins with knowing where you are headed. Today your destination is aspirational in nature as your arrival most likely will seem out of reach to you. No worries, make the first step today on your great healing adventure by beginning to apply the ideas and suggestions in this book to your life. Remember to allow the necessary time for your healing efforts to marinate within you as you make sense and come to grips with this gift of life you possess. Welcome aboard, your destination may take time, but the HEALING PROCESS starts today and will be evident throughout your journey.

Truths from the Road: Your Healing Destination

"It means to continue to do the normal things in life."

"For me it is expanding my social circle, learning to be social again."

"Not to be sad all the time."

"To get my bounce back."

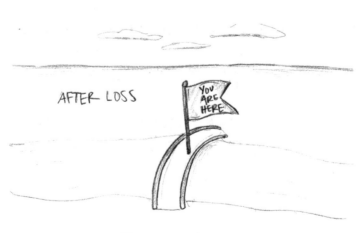

You Are Here. Stuff Happened.

How lucky I am to have known somebody and something that saying goodbye is so damned awful.

—Evans G. Valens,
The Other Side of the Mountain: The Story of Jill Kinmont

Blindsided by Loss?

Nothing is so painful to the human mind as a great and sudden change.

—Mary Wollstonecraft Shelley, *Frankenstein*

Were you "so blindsided" and "in shock" by your loss? Even if you were intellectually prepared for your loss, the size and scope of your loss feels like being emotionally blindsided. Grievers tell me they had "no idea" how hard this loss was going to be on them. It is not uncommon for grievers to think they will work through their grief in a few weeks or a few months. Many realize later that their loss is a tough taskmaster and healing will take more time and attention than they anticipated. All loss can be traumatic. Those who have experienced both kinds of loss say, "I don't know which was better," a sudden loss or a loss from a long debilitating disease or illness. The common denominator for either type of loss is the visceral full effect of being blindsided. One man reported he was driving home from running an errand soon after his loss when "all of a sudden it hit me, Susan is not there (home). I hyperventilated Catching my breath, I said to myself, 'Susan is gone forever.' A thunderbolt right through my heart." *Blindsided.*

Is This Your Life's Greatest Challenge?

Dying is a wild Night and a new Road.

—Emily Dickinson

Your loss may be the defining moment in your life. The death of an essential person in your life may redefine who you are and chart the trajectory of the rest of your life. In fact, we call it, Life Before and Life After. It may feel like you are a victim of a *hit and run* as one grieving woman stated, "For me, the feeling of grief is 'Hit and Run' and I am left in shambles." When I ask, "Is this your life's greatest challenge?" in group settings, the answer is invariably a resounding and universal yes. In previous challenges your loved one was by your side to help guide and support. Many bereaved who were long-term caregivers for their loved one, have stated that "this is the tougher of the two journeys." Even with their loved one in diminished health, grievers report that *hope* was always there even until the very end. For many bereaved, this is the first time they have ever lived alone in their lives, a great challenge, especially in advancing years. One man stated after the recent loss of his wife, "I've never hurt like this in my life." Another asked, "What is happening to me?"

Your loss may have resulted in your life's biggest change ever. This could very possibly be the hardest work you will ever do. You are going to need a great road map.

Two Commonly Asked Questions

Will I ever *feel* normal?

Will I ever *be* normal?

The answers to these questions are: YES and YES.

After significant loss, I am convinced that there are four universal truths that can provide us a framework to build on moving forward. For me, the entire grief process can be distilled into these four truths.

The Four Truths after Loss

1. Your loved one will be in your heart for the rest of your life.
2. You are one of the lucky ones to have fully loved AND to have been fully loved.
3. You owe it to your loved one's legacy to move forward in life.
4. You will find joy again knowing that some of your best days are still ahead.

What Grief Teaches Us: To Exist or to Live

In three words, I can sum up everything I've learned about life. It goes on.

—Robert Frost

We often hear that grief is a great teacher. The great American poet Robert Frost reminds us that life after loss continues, "it goes on." Yes, life does go on, but what is grief teaching us?

- Is grief teaching us to exist only or is it teaching us to live fully?
- Grief has changed our lives, and we should not want to waste this hurt, this painful lesson.
- Loss and grief provide opportunities to grow, learn, and make something positive out of the ravages of loss.

I hope you choose the ROAD TO LIVE FULLY and to continue on this journey together, this great adventure.

18

We all know the axiom that life has two absolutes you can count on: death and taxes. If we are fortunate to have loved and lost, then we need to add love and grief to the mix. If there is death with love, grief follows. It is nearly impossible to get through life without grief, grieving the loss of someone or something of great value to you. It only makes sense that if you love, you will be "taxed" at your loved one's death. Over time, I am hopeful you will see that any "grief taxes" imposed will be small compared to the *return* of the love that you have received and enjoyed, and the love that is everlasting.

Grief, the Great Disrupter

Grief is very disruptive. Death changes everything. Not just the loss of the life of your loved one, but in so many related areas of your life. Like the ripples caused by a stone hitting the surface of the water, the changes from your loss seem to reach far and wide. In the early days of grief, grievers have reported: "My life is over" or "I have nothing to live for" or "My life is on quicksand." In these early days, hopelessness can be prevalent. Death can open our eyes to viewing life as precious. That is why we need to design our own road map for our future after loss—to make the most of the rest of our lives. Perhaps you now find yourself asking, What now? What's next?

What Now? What's Next?

Grief is in two parts. The first is loss. The second is the remaking of life.
                                        —Anne Roiphe, *Epilogue*

Welcoming Your New Crossroads

Your present is represented by your loss and your progression to a future will be represented by your road map. You are in the present, currently at the crossroads experiencing great change from your loss. As you design your road map, you will begin to understand the roads that will help lead you through grief, to healing and renewal. Which road will you take?

The bereaved have taught me that "there's no handbook for this." One bereaved spouse told me regarding the loss of her husband, "Well, they tell me, this is a new chapter in my life, that I will need to write *The Book of Olivia*." Since grief does not come with an instruction guide, let's work together to craft a road map. We know that it will not be perfect, but perhaps it will be exactly what you need to get *on the road* to healing.

Your Plan B Road Map

Your Plan A for the future was to have your loved one by your side. Unfortunately, your loss means Plan A is no longer available to you.

"I want my life back" and "I just want things to be like they used to be."

This is a variation on a common refrain. Sorry, but we will need to work on Plan B together. Plan B is not what life *used* to be or what life *should* be, but what life *will be* in your new future, as you begin to build your new life afresh on a solid foundation. The distance from Plan A to Plan B is simply the distance from Point A, where you are today, to Point B, your *destination of renewal*.

Hope, Trust, and Aspiration: Essential Travel Companions

> God puts rainbows in the clouds so that each of us—in the dreariest and most dreaded moments—can see a possibility of hope.
> —Maya Angelou

> "Hope" is the thing with feathers—That perches in the soul—And sings the tunes without the words—And never stops—at all.
> —Emily Dickinson

The very least you can do in your life is figure out what you hope for. And the most you can do is live inside that hope. Not admire it from a distance, but live right in it, under its roof.

—Barbara Kingsolver, *Animal Dreams*

This Book Is about Hope

It's that simple. Without hope we are destined to be stuck in grief. Grief is meant to be a temporary place for a season of life that we move through, not our permanent home. I like to think the hope we will express is authentic and comes with our feet firmly planted on terra firma rather than a Pollyanna "pie in the sky" concept of hope. Perhaps we need to view hope in a new, fresh way. Hope repackaged, hope redefined, hope reframed with you in mind. Hope is what happens when you have a *road map*, a *plan* and a *process*, and the confidence that no matter the circumstances, you possess the ability to be content and experience joy and happiness again!

. . . and Aspiration

To aspire means hoping to accomplish a goal in the future. Many of the ideas and suggestions presented in the following pages are aspirational in nature. Perhaps some of these ideas, tools, and suggestions are there for you to bank and store in escrow until you are ready to try them on for size. Please plan to revisit these healing concepts when you are ready. We all need something in which to aspire and you are in charge of your timetable. Go at your own pace and be sure to adjust and modify your road map as you move forward.

Truths from the Road: HOPE . . . and Trust

Trust that our hope for our new future will be fulfilled. Trust that our situation will improve and trust that we will reach our destination of being fully alive again. Trust the process of transformation. One man told me, "I know I'm going to get my life back again, but it sure will look different."

Hope to "continue to grow and do the things I'm dreaming of."
Hope that "I can forgive myself."
Hope "to find companionship."
Hope "to have joy and serenity in this new chapter of my life."

Reframing "Moving Forward"

If you can't fly, run; if you can't run, walk; if you can't walk, crawl; but by all means keep moving.

—Martin Luther King, Jr.

The only cure for grief is action.

—George Henry Lewes

Getting over a painful experience is much like crossing monkey bars. You have to let go at some point in order to move forward.

—Unknown

How Do We Define "Moving Forward"?

Among those grieving, the phrase "moving on" is often cited as one of the least helpful and most offensive phrases they hear after their loss. Many of the bereaved I work with tell me their greatest complaint is people telling them to "move on" or "get over it." Sometimes it is well-meaning friends; sometimes it is family members, neighbors, or work colleagues. No doubt you may have been given this advice, and you may be hesitant to "move forward" because of how you define moving forward. Simply stated, many who grieve often associate moving on with abandoning and forgetting the memory of their loved one. Moving on can give the impression of a lack of love or respect for the deceased. I have heard the bereaved say: "I want to stay and live with the comfort of my grief" or "If I give up my grief, I feel like I'm giving up on my loved one."

We need to reframe how we view the phrase "moving forward" after loss. For healthy grieving we need to move forward, but *move forward without forgetting* and keep our loved ones in our hearts forever. The best examples of healthy grieving involve moving forward in a thoughtful and sensitive way to keep the memory and legacy of the loved one alive while moving forward with new experiences and building a new life without the physical presence of the loved one.

Death changes more than the loss of our loved one, it also changes us. With change comes movement. Are we moving forward or backwards? Are we stuck in grief? One man told me, "I don't want to be like my aunt. After she lost her husband she just got stuck in her grief and became a bitter woman for the last twenty years of her life." Perhaps we should redefine "moving forward" as a flexible and everchanging concept that best describes you today. And revisit it tomorrow, and the day after, and so forth. Whether you know it or not, or acknowledge it, you will be moving forward, even though for some the pace and breadth of the movement may not seem noticeable.

Is Moving Forward Letting Go?

No, for us to move forward, we will never forget the impact on our lives that our loved one has; this stays in our hearts forever unchanged. This has not been "let go." Yes, moving forward is letting go of the false concept that "I don't deserve to be happy again" or "I am not worthy" to fully engage and live again and laugh again. It is *yes* to letting go of any survivor guilt. I have heard countless stories from the bereaved wishing they had died rather than the loved ones. Some express the following: "I expected it would be me to go first" and "I would have changed places with my wife in a heartbeat," or "I offered the doctor to take my organs if they would help." No, moving forward is honoring both our loved one and life itself, by making the most of the days we have left on this earth.

EPIPHANY ALERT: No Choice but to Move Forward

As human beings we are hard-wired to have a strong will to live. No matter how severely our foundation has been rocked, our will to live remains strong. We have no choice but to move forward. If we sit on a bike and do not move, we will fall over. If thrown in a swimming pool, we will drown if we do not move. It takes no more effort to use our arms and legs to swim than to tread water. It is about movement, combined with intentional reflection to move forward to our destination of healing and our new future.

The Decision

I take to the open road, healthy, free, the world before me
—Walt Whitman, "Song of the Open Road"

The road is there, it will always be there. You just have to decide when to take it.
—Chris Humphrey

Congratulations, you've said yes to moving forward! You have answered the bell to take up the challenge to move forward. Congratulations for having the interest to learn, heal, laugh, cry, and have hope for a future; some of your best days lay ahead. You are now different. You are the same. Life was not perfect before your loss. Life will not be perfect moving forward. But you are resilient, designed to take a blow. I applaud your decision to move forward with your life.

EPIPHANY ALERT: The Secret of Healing

Growing to give is the secret to healing. A reason to grow is that you will have something to give. If you learn the lesson of giving by helping others, you will continue to grow on your road to healing. You must move forward to grow, give, and heal.

Theodor Seuss Geisel reminds us in his well-loved children's book, *Oh, the Places You'll Go!* that we have all that we need to move forward—we have brains, feet, and can steer ourselves in any direction we choose. And Dr. Seuss lets us know that we will succeed: "98 and ¾ percent guaranteed." I think this applies to the road to your new future. Start, don't just *think* about starting. Do, don't just think about doing.

As you read, skip over sections that do not apply or come back to them, whenever they do apply. You are in charge. So, travel at your own pace. This is not meant as one more thing for your overtaxed brain and heart to cope with, but simply to aid in your journey, your quest for feeling normal again, and being able to survive and then thrive, even without the love of your life (or someone for whom you deeply cared).

Bon voyage! Wishing you, as it literally means in French, a "good journey."

Opportunity Ahead

One doesn't discover new lands without consenting to lose sight, for a very long time, of the shore.

—André Gide

The only way to make sense out of change is to plunge into it, move with it, and join the dance.

—Alan Watts

In the middle of difficulty lies opportunity.

—Albert Einstein

ROAD SCHOLAR
ASSIGNMENT: Self-audit

Take a personal inventory or self-audit today. Let your mind wander and visualize where you are today and where you would like to be with your life in the future. Write quickly, and write as if no one is looking, because no one is! These are your private thoughts and are not the property of anyone else. And be honest with yourself. Remember to return at your discretion, in three, six, or twelve months to review and revise according to what you have learned about yourself.

Today's Date: _____

1. How would you describe your current physical, mental, and emotional well-being?
2. How would you describe your family/social relationships today?
3. Describe what an ideal situation in your future would look like?

Start Your Engines!

Your inspiration awaits . . .
Your passion awaits . . .
Your motivation awaits . . .

Your opportunity awaits . . . and is ready for the taking. It may seem counterintuitive, but *inspiration, passion,* and *motivation* are all best found by *doing.* Like low-hanging fruit, grab it now. Traditional thinking is that we should wait until inspiration strikes us, or wait until we discover what we are passionate about. Then we will be motivated and throw ourselves into a worthwhile and meaningful project or task. DOING is best accomplished by knowing our opportunities.

You should think of opportunity as the fuel that will drive you forward on your road trip beyond grief. The Latin origin of the word *opportunity* comes from "favorable winds." This simply means that when certain circumstances come together or are present then the possibility for something important is poised to happen.

Opportunity Ahead: Stretch? Grow? Open to Change?

Imagine: Beauty out of the ashes of loss. Opportunities for growth? One woman told me, "I never imagined I would be doing all the things I do now after my husband's death." Another said, "Regrets be damned, no more regrets" and another "I have learned from grief to 'seize the day' and that life is short, no regrets." Full steam ahead!

Where Does This Opportunity for Personal Growth Reside?

It is already here, inside and all around you, just waiting to be picked up and tried on for size. You have been given a blank canvas, what will you create? *You have the opportunity to view your life afresh again.* People grow after loss, and can become stronger, more resilient, and more open to change and growth. You will too!

Opportunity in Plain Sight

As you read the following pages, do some soul-searching for that "something" that resonates with you, that interests or inspires you. Expect to encounter a spark of an idea that you will want to bring to life. You may not be ready for it, but you can let yourself and the world around you know that this is something you would like to start working on or do when the time is right and you are ready. Let it marinate. Sometimes your opportunity is there waiting for you, in plain sight.

Truths from the Road— Opportunity

I can eat peas again," stated one woman whose husband could not stand the smell of peas.

"I am now able to travel, not looking after my spouse, I can visit my out-of-state family."

True Grit: The Oyster and the Pearl

Don't underestimate the grit that you carry within you. It is that grit you possess that will help you on your road to growth and healing. Remember it is that lowly piece of grit, that grain of sand that makes an oyster able to produce a pearl. Is that piece of grit you are carrying within, your grief? If so, then even your uncomfortable grief is capable of producing good things over time, perhaps even your symbolic pearl. Is it possible that some good, some growth, can come from your loss? What would it take for you to believe—enthusiastically—that some of "the best days" of your life are still ahead?

Time: The Challenging Opportunity

Learning to adjust to having additional time on your hands as a result of your loss can be difficult. Making good use of this time is certainly challenging but also an opportunity. One man told me, "I went from not having thirty minutes free to being 24/7 free." A common response for those grieving is that they throw themselves into keeping busy. "If I stay busy, I don't have to think about it." In the following sections on DOING and BEING you will find constructive strategies for managing this bonus of extra time.

The Opportunity Paradox

Your loved one's death may have created a set of circumstances that makes it possible to do something which had been out of your reach, that is opportunity. At the same time, your loved one's death creates an inertia, a true fog, and a condition we call "grief brain," meaning you are not "firing on all cylinders" which makes it harder to act on this new set of circumstances known as opportunity.

Truths from the Road:
Future Plans

"I am planning to take in a student boarder to live downstairs to help with expenses and provide some direction and companionship."

"I am planning to complete 10K walks that go through the capitol buildings of all fifty states."

Opportunity Road Map: What Should I Do with the Rest of My Life?

Naturally, the simple answer is "enjoy it," but to enjoy life, especially after a tough loss, can be incredibly difficult. Please view the road ahead as your

OPPORTUNITY ROAD MAP as we continue to work together to help you find joy and meaning again in your life.

ROAD SCHOLAR ASSIGNMENT: Create Your Interest/ Bucket List

A bucket list is a very common approach to ensure that we make the most of our lives while we still can. One woman stated, "I don't have a bucket, let alone a list." Well, here's your chance. Take a moment to write down five things you have always wanted to do but have not done, or would like to try again. Or list a place you would like to visit or revisit. After your loss, your interest/bucket list most likely will have changed, so be sure to include what is important to you now.

MILEPOST TIP: Opportunity Knocking

Consider adding any of the following tips to your journey.

#1 Be Open to Opportunity

Be open to opportunities that weren't available earlier to you before your loss. Accept invitations to a movie or dinner. Open your eyes to disguised opportunities, often imperfect situations that lead to a more fulfilling future for you.

#2 Give Yourself Permission to Pursue an Opportunity

No matter how small, or what others may think, give yourself permission to pursue an opportunity. Sometimes your true direction will be revealed once you are on the road of opportunity.

#3 Let Your Pendulum Swing Opportunity

With your loss, your pendulum has swung completely to one side as far as possible. If you want to get back to feeling normal, your "new normal," then your pendulum must be allowed space to swing back.

#4 Perspective and Wisdom Opportunity

If you are fortunate to have friends and mentors in your life, be sure to take advantage of this important resource. Seek their insights and perspectives. They know you and want the best for you and may be able to help you see the broader horizon for your road ahead.

#5 How to Resist an Unwanted Opportunity

Just say NO. If saying no is difficult for you, then couch your answer with a softer qualifying response but still firmly no. Thank the person for the offer. You can say something like "Thank you for thinking of me but at this time I am not interested." As a newly bereaved person you may receive unwelcome solicitations from well-meaning friends and family trying to shoehorn you into opportunities that are not life giving or satisfying to you. Be sure to use the adage of not making major decisions for the first year in these situations.

#6 Go with the Pull: The Push-Pull Theory of Opportunity

In life we often do not leave our comfort zones without a push. Perhaps your loss is the push that life has given you. Whether you like it or not, change has happened in your life, that is your *push*. I like to think that growth and new experiences, your Road Map Beyond Grief, is the *pull*. You've experienced the push, now be prepared to embrace the pull. *Go with the pull.*

#7 The Opportunity to be Surprised by Joy

When joy fell by the wayside with your loss, the last thing you may have imagined was that you could expect joy to once again enter your life. On this journey, hopefully, you will begin to experience fleeting moments of joy at first, and over time, become fully surprised by joy on a daily basis.

Call of the Road: Why a Road Trip?

> *. . . the road is life*
>
> —Jack Kerouac, *On the Road*

> *I travel not to go anywhere, but to go. I travel for travel's sake. The great affair is to move.*
>
> —Robert Louis Stevenson

"Begin at the beginning,, the King said gravely, "and go on till you come to the end: then stop."

—Lewis Carroll, *Alice's Adventures in Wonderland*

A year from now you may wish you had started today.

—Karen Lamb

Welcome to the Road!

metaphor (noun)

Definition as cited by *The Merriam-Webster Dictionary*:

met-a-phor 1 : a *figure of speech* in which a word or phrase literally denoting one kind of object or idea is used in place of another to suggest a likeness or analogy between them (as in *drowning in money*).

If a journey is often described as a metaphor for life, it is no stretch to enlist the ROAD and your ROAD TRIP as the metaphor of choice for your grief journey. Your road trip is a metaphor for your new life ahead beyond grief. A metaphor enables you to add a visual component to your grief journey, so you can picture or visualize your healing destination. So, is The Road a journey or destination? It is both. Healing from loss and grief is both a journey and a destination. The actual process of participating in the journey is healing in itself, but we want to be destination people. We want to make sure we know where we are going, so that each of us reaches our appropriate, unique destination. Welcome to *The Road*—your safe journey to healing and your new personal life direction.

Ode to the Road

The roads of *Loss, Grief,* and *Bereavement* all lead to change. This book is designed to equip you with the ability to embrace the changes you are facing today and learn how to navigate these changes that were thrust upon you. By definition a journey implies movement, from one point to another. Grief is often described as a journey. Just as a health diagnosis often leads to the language of "cancer journey" or "health journey," reading this book suggests you or a loved one are on a "grief journey." Since the beginning of time, people have embarked on journeys, from Homer's *Odyssey* to the Israelites forty-year journey to the promised land, to countless journeys to find new lands, to find riches, and to travel to holy sites on pilgrimages. Whatever the reason, a journey means moving forward, putting one foot in front of the other and heading down a path ahead or traveling on the road ahead. To embark on a journey, two things need to happen: first, the *decision* to move forward has to be made, and second, the *act* of moving forward has to be made. I truly believe that in many ways grievers are on a "heroic journey."

Truths from the Road— My Grief Journey Metaphor

"My grief journey feels like a bridge over the river separating life from death."

"Mine is a tornado, with everything broken in sight."

"My metaphor is time. I didn't lose my wife, I just ran out of time."

"My journey metaphor is a great tree, with the trunk being my marriage, and now I am sprouting a branch, to branch out. When the leaves fall, they serve as mulch to help the tree grow."

Choosing Your Destination

A journey needs a destination. Your destination is unique to you, but it includes the healing properties of arriving home, to be at peace with yourself. Your destination is the rediscovery of joy again, to feel normal again, and to set or at least allow a new personal life direction after loss. Do you have the courage to set your destination? Do you have faith, hope, and trust that you can set your personal direction? Chances are you may be stalled, stuck, or lacking the energy to even think about it. That is OK for now. Keep putting one foot ahead of the other and your destination will open up to you. Enjoy the journey, the healing is in the journey as much as in the destination.

A journey needs a road map. A road map may offer many routes to your destination. Did you know, according to the Federal Highway Administration, that there are over four million miles of paved roads in the United States alone? Similarly, there is a world of roads waiting for you to chart your own way as you design your road map to your new future.

Choosing Your Road Trip

Embrace change. You have no choice, as change is in the air. I chose the road trip as a metaphor for your adventure through and beyond grief to your new destination.

31

- The road trip is our chosen mode of travel, our specific vehicle of choice to move you through and beyond your grieving.

- The road trip represents the balm, or healing agent, for your loss.

- A road trip illustrates movement, a road trip is something in which we all can identify. A road trip brings memories and the prospect of new experiences which can prove challenging as well as healing and therapeutic.

- A road trip mirrors a grief journey in many ways. You have the ability to stop and start at your convenience. You have the opportunity to stay longer, or leave earlier than expected, and the option to explore new surroundings.

- On this road trip adventure, we may need to do some digging, to excavate some of the hidden interests, talents, and dreams that may have been buried since your youth.

Expect the unexpected, but plan/commit to move forward and make progress, despite speed bumps, potholes, and road closures ahead. Expect to be surprised by awesome vistas with sunsets, sunrises, rainbows, and stunning natural scenery at your disposal until you reach your destination. The GREAT SECRET is that once you begin your journey, your road trip to hope and healing, you will begin to experience glimpses of your destination.

ROAD SCHOLAR ASSIGNMENT: Create Your At-a-Glance Road Map

Take out a sheet of blank paper, fold to make a three-panel sheet. This is your road map. Take thirty minutes to complete the following.

The Three-Panel Road Map

Panel 1: YOU ARE HERE. List attributes of how you see yourself today, your strengths and weaknesses.

Panel 2: OPPORTUNITIES/BARRIERS AHEAD. What opportunities and barriers lay ahead?

Panel 3: DESTINATION. What characteristics are you looking for in your destination? A new go-to person, new interests, companionship, travel, considering a change?

Extra credit for drawings, adding photos or clippings out of magazines, and annotated notes on your road map. Place your name on it with today's date with your signature. This is your commitment to yourself to use, revise, and come back to review in the year ahead.

Road Readiness: Understanding Your Road Trip

First Rule of the Road: Never pass up an opportunity to pee.
—Unknown

"Would you tell me, please, which way I ought to go from here?"
"That depends a good deal on where you want to get to,"
said the Cat.
"I don't much care where –" said Alice.
"Then it doesn't much matter which way you go," said the Cat.

—Lewis Carroll, *Alice's Adventures in Wonderland*

Road Trip Requirements

- A plan, where you want to go. Your destination.
- A road map, showing you how to get there.
- What to bring, baggage you want to *take* and *leave* behind.
- Reliable transportation, for you to be in good working order, personal wellness.

Rules of the Road

1. **There Are No Shortcuts:** There is no speed grief, there is no "grief lite." There is no estimated time of arrival (ETA).

2. **You Have À La Carte Permission:** You have permission at any time, without shame, to put this book down and pick it up when ready or to skip to those parts that are helpful to you. As your perspective on grief changes over time, you may want to revisit skipped over parts when you are more receptive and have more energy.

3. **Expect Delays and Challenges:** Barriers and obstacles from the past and future will be real but surmountable. Backsliding is optional.

4. **OK to EXIT:** There are EXITS on this road trip, and it is OK to exit at any time. I call this hitting the PAUSE button.

5. **No U-Turn Allowed:** You are free to move forward imperfectly, and sideways, and even backwards on occasion, but no full U-turn on your road to your new you.

6. **Choose Your Own Metaphor:** If you wish, you may want to substitute another interest you have for the road. Perhaps you may see your process of renewal and reinvention as building a house, and substitute a blueprint for a road map, or perhaps keep the concept of movement, but change your mode of travel to sailing or flying. You decide.

7. **The Road Is Your Future:** Embrace the road. It is life.

Truths from the Road: Travel Advice from Grievers for Grievers

"You will find those whose only message is 'get back on the horse' and those who will nurture you and be willing to be present with your pain. Both are good and valuable to you. There will be times when you are too raw to be with motivators and times when the nurturer will just slow your forward movement down. Try to be aware and in control of what you need and when you need it."

Travel Advice: Instruction Notes

This is your journey, travel at your pace, expect to get lost at times, but know that you will find your way back to your road map to your future. Your Road Trip is not a journey to rush, or simply to eat up the miles, as getting to your destination requires time to *discover* yourself along the road as a bonus to your healing and becoming whole again.

- **Who Are We?** We look like everyone else, but we are different. We have been changed by loss. Perhaps you may want to think of yourself, for now, as a Grief Traveler, Grief Tripper, "Road" Scholar, or Road Pilgrim. Grieving is not something you simply want to discard, leave behind—it is a legitimate part of your life during this journey.

- **What's Next? Your Future.** Did you know? As human beings we are the only species that contemplates the future.

- **Expect Speed Bumps and Slow Progress.** Expect a few delays, the speed bumps and potholes are merely those gotchas, those grief bursts, grief ambushes, or grief land mines that coexist with us on this road. Do not be disappointed if you do not see immediate progress, that is normal. Remember, one step at a time, if not one mile at a time, then a half mile at a time.

- **Expect Change: You Will Change on Your Road Trip.** Your grief will change and evolve over time, your heart will evolve as well. Be patient but be expectant of growth.

- **Filling Station Ahead.** Fill yourself with grace—grace not to be hard on yourself for your slower than hoped for progress, grace to overlook people who are annoying or troublesome to you. Offer grace to yourself and to those around you.

- **Expect to Travel through Strange and "Foreign" Lands.** After loss, you may encounter new lands "foreign" to you, such as anger, guilt, pride, and impatience. When you identify such a land, name it and acknowledge it and put this land on notice that it will not be a permanent detour for you. Once you have done that, thank these foreign lands for what they have taught you and move forward on your journey.

   ROAD THERAPY: The Road Is Your Healing. The lure of the road, even the mental imagery of the road, can be therapeutic. Big sky above, open road ahead, changing and evolving landscapes, the vastness of scale, a perspective of something greater than yourself. Did you know you have at your disposal millions of miles of paved roads, highways, interstates, and scenic overlooks to explore and find yourself. Fasten your seat belt and enjoy the ride.

ROAD VISUALIZATION: You Are Your Car

Everything in life is somewhere else, and you get there in a car.

—E. B. White, "Fro-Joy" in *One Man's Meat*

Grief is hard work. How about allowing yourself a lighthearted "just for fun" moment? If you want, enjoy this chapter of visualization escape. If not interested, keep on moving. Give yourself permission to look at your loss with a fresh set of eyes.

For a moment, let's allow ourselves to be represented as a car. A car is a symbol of freedom and independence. A car can take any road and is able to go short or long distances. Let's imagine for a moment assigning automotive names to our human selves. Perhaps the following might look like this:

The Dashboard: Your Brain

The Engine: Your Heart

The Chassis: Your Body

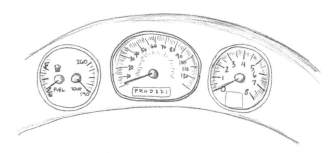

What Is Your Dashboard Telling You?

How are you doing according to your dashboard? Where are you today?

- What gear are you in?

- Are you in Park? Are you in Neutral? Do you think you are in Reverse? With the gear shift description of PRNDSL, you may find yourself in one of the first three gear selections: Park, Reverse, and Neutral. Try beginning your journey with the final three gear selections, starting with Low, moving to Slow, and finally to Drive.

- What is your GPS setting? Which direction is your internal GPS pointing? Set your GPS (Grieving Person Syndrome) coordinates to healing and trust you will find your way through grief.

- What's in your tank?

- Running on empty? What is your E/F fuel gauge telling you? No doubt your fuel tank is depleted after your loss. I often hear "I have nothing left in the tank" and "I am running on fumes." If your tank is low, I hope you will find opportunities from the suggestions in the following pages to refill your tank.

ROAD SCHOLAR ASSIGNMENT: What Is Your Dashboard Telling You?

Take a reading of where you are today. Revisit it at your convenience.

Gear: Reverse to Park/Neutral to Low Gear: Which gear am I?

Gear: _____

Fuel Tank: Empty to Full: What do I have in my tank?

Fuel Tank: _____

GPS/Compass: Which direction am I headed?

Compass/GPS:_____ _

Temperature: What is my emotional temperature?

Temperature Setting: _____

Odometer: How far have I come? How much farther do I still want to go?

Odometer: _____

Truths from the Road: You Are Your Dashboard

"I am a gearshift and I am in neutral, just coasting."

"I am the gas pedal, so I can go faster but I also have a foot on the brake as well."

"I am a rear-view mirror, to see things more clearly, and to look back to the past with my husband."

"I am a check engine light bulb, to make sure all is OK with the engine, that when applied to life, to make sure all is well today and in my future planning."

"I am my fuel gauge, it fluctuates. It was between empty and half full but over the weekend and feeling lonely it ebbed back to empty, now it moving toward full being in our group today."

BAGGAGE: What's in Your Baggage?

We come fully equipped from the factory. We have lungs, we can breathe. We have brains, we can think. We have hearts, we can feel empathy. We can move. The rest is a bonus. We are alive, and in the words of Neil Pasricha, if we are alive—"we have won the lottery."

WHAT TO BRING ON THE ROAD: Your Road Trip Packing List

Become a Road Scholar. Become a student of the road and bring your curiosity, interests, and your willingness to be "surprised by joy." Consider bringing the following "positive" baggage. If not now, look for opportunities to add these important companions.

- Open heart
- Open mind
- Open to change
- Open to laughter
- Open to hope
- Open to a higher power

BAGGAGE: What Not to Bring

No *unwanted* and *unnecessary* baggage allowed! We all carry mental and emotional baggage, and after your loss expect these bags to grow in size and weight. Some baggage is meant to stay home.

DO-NOT-BRING LIST: Do Leave Home without It, Please!

The following are unwanted or unnecessary baggage that will stall you on your road to healing:

- Feeling "I am not worthy of moving forward"
- Unrealistic grieving timeline/ETA
- Stress/Anxiety
- Worry/Fear
- Regret
- Guilt/Survivor Guilt
- Anger/Unforgiveness
- Hopelessness

What unnecessary baggage are you carrying?

NO PANIC, NO WORRIES: Small Carry-ons Allowed

It will be virtually impossible to not bring at least "small" bags of the above. If you bring it, prepare to jettison as much as you can as soon as possible. There will be opportunities to leave some of your unwanted baggage as we move forward on the road ahead.

What New "Bags" Do I Hope to Add on the Road?

- Make new friends or reconnect with old friends?
- Discover new interests or hobbies?
- Learn new skills?
- Add resilience?
- Add endurance?
- Add strength?
- Add grace?

What other "bag" do you want to add?

Truths from the Road: The Baggage of Grief

The Shock

"It still came as a shock even though the end had been in sight."

"I thought we had more time."

"I was hoping for another two, three, five years."

The Effects of Loss

"My brain is a sieve."

"After my loss, I feel like I am half of the whole."

"It is an overwhelming cloud that hangs over you . . . forever."

Living on Less after Loss

"Money is an issue. We spent our nest egg on his health care and now I am afraid I will have to move."

"I was told by our accountant that I will need to get a part time job, even at my age."

Loss of Identity

"I don't feel like myself anymore, I feel like I am half of a person, half of what I used to be."

"I don't know who I am."

"Fifty years of we and now it's just me."

Multiple Losses

"Second game of a doubleheader," said one man after the death of his second wife, *"new lineup, new pitcher, another loss."*

"Our first child died at seventeen months. There is no comparison to this, losing my wife. Our child's death brought us closer together. Such a tragedy usually breaks up a couple."

Map Planning: Understanding Your Road Map

We're all pilgrims on the same journey—but some pilgrims have better road maps.

—Nelson DeMille

You know more of a road by having traveled it than by all the conjectures and descriptions in the world.

—William Hazlitt

There's a lot of optimism in changing scenery, in seeing what's down the road.

—Conor Oberst

Goal/Purpose of This Road Map

A road map is a plan, and a plan can make us feel better. A road map can show us that we do have a future and that it is possible to feel normal again. A road map is the tool we use to help us get from point A to point B, or after loss, to help us get from PLAN A to PLAN B. A road map can help get us out of the parking space after a devastating loss, and help us bounce back, and ultimately bounce forward.

Moving from A to B will not be a straight line, but it will be forward progress. I ask that you be patient and remain open minded and flexible as you move forward. Progress on your grief journey is not always easily identifiable. Your road map is your guide to navigate your future, your road ahead through and beyond grief to hope and healing, to find joy again.

A Journey for All Seasons

Your road map to the future no doubt will include personal direction that is both seasonal and long lasting.

Expect people to come into this season of your life. Be open to and on the lookout for those who will be incredibly helpful to you, even though, at first glance, it may appear you have nothing in common. Let people step in the gap, and allow yourself to receive help or kindness, as you will be a blessing to them to allow them to be able to serve you. Likewise, you will discover that an important part of your healing will occur when you find yourself in a position to help others who may be struggling with what you are going through today. *Paying it forward.*

As we age, we understand there are seasons in life. You have had or are navigating a season of loss. You have seen loss *up close and personal* and this book is intended to focus on your new season, the season of living. Everything in life has a season, this we learn from the Book of Ecclesiastes:

To every thing there is a season,

and a time to every purpose under the heaven:

A time to be born, a time to die;
a time to plant, and a time to pluck up that which is planted;
A time to kill, and a time to heal;
a time to break down, and a time to build up;
A time to weep, and a time to laugh;
a time to mourn, and a time to dance;
A time to cast away stones, and a time to gather stones together;
a time to embrace, and a time to refrain from embracing;
A time to get, and a time to lose;
a time to keep, and a time to cast away;
A time to rend, and a time to sew;
a time to keep silence, and a time to speak;
A time to love, and a time to hate;
A time of war, and a time of peace.

—Ecclesiastes 3:1–8, KJV

Journal Thoughts _____

_____

_____

_____

_____

_____

_____

_____

_____

_____

_____

_____

_____

_____

_____

ROAD SCHOLAR ASSIGNMENT: Wall-to-Wall Road Mapping

Let's get visual. Find a bulletin board, the back side of a door, or the side of a refrigerator and consider one or more of the following options to get a visual image of your new personal life direction.

- **Sticky Note Wall Poster:** Divide a poster board into three sections, NOW, SOON, FUTURE.
- From the Interest/Bucket List assignment, take your list of things you have always wanted to do or the interests you may want to explore. Use sticky notes since they can be moved to a different date.
  - **NOW:** Add sticky notes with ideas written on them for you to try in the next week or two. See the DOING section for inspiration.
  - **SOON:** Add sticky notes for you to try thirty–sixty days from now.
  - **FUTURE:** Add sticky notes for any long-range goals. What you aspire or hope to be doing in six, nine, or twelve months or more in the future.
- **Wall Poster Calendar:** Divide a poster board into four sections, WINTER, SPRING, SUMMER, FALL, or twelve sections, for the months of the year.
  - Use sticky note place holders on your wall calendar as mileposts or mile markers.
  - Place important "gotcha" dates on your calendar, such as anniversaries including "deathiversaries," birthdays, and celebrated occasions and holidays. By doing so, you will be able to plan a strategy in advance for each of these dates. Over time each date will become less of a landmine to step on than a treasured memory to cherish.
- **"Momentum" Wall Calendar:** Purchase a large 365-day wall calendar or make one with 365 boxes. Begin today, put a large check mark or red X on each day that you made one baby step forward on your road map journey. This will be a visual reminder of how many baby steps you have made and will help develop your momentum. You can use stickers or any other creative option available. Give yourself permission to use a "time out" or "off-the-grid" mark for those days you are not feeling up to the task. Permission granted.

Weathering the "Big Storm"

You have weathered the "big storm" of loss. Perhaps you knew your storm was coming. Perhaps you were able to prepare to some degree, but now you are living in the aftermath of this great storm. The skies may not have cleared from your loss, and you no doubt have or will encounter that grief fog, with your "grief brain" clouding your vision and perception. Keep in mind, as you travel this road, no matter the weather outside, your internal weather will be gradually improving as you move forward.

How Do You Wish to Travel?

After loss, we would all like the road ahead to be straight forward. We know that it is nothing like that. Sometimes grief is described as a hurricane, twisting and swirling in circles even as it moves forward. Many grievers find grief is like being on a "merry go-round and I can't get off." Your road trip ahead may be smooth or it may feel like "being on a roller coaster that is moving forward." Your road map not only takes you through beautiful and inspiring terrain but also through tough neighborhoods.

Know Your Signs Ahead

You may or may not encounter delays, detours, or roadblocks, but the following are some potential slowdowns you may face and strategies to help you cope. Your road trip to healing will not be trouble free. Expect to *navigate* difficult terrain. Expect some challenging stretches of road. Expect roadblocks, speed bumps, and a detour or two that may be challenging to you. You decide which of these detours you need to take, and those  you can bypass to keep moving forward. Ideally, your destination road to healing may come to look like the progression of road signs above.

A Journey for All Speeds

He that lacks time to mourn, lacks time to mend.

—Sir Henry Taylor, "Philipe van Artevelde"

It does not matter how slowly you go, so long as you do not stop.

—Confucius

In the world in which we live, we want speed, so, naturally, we would prefer *speed grieving*. However, we know instinctively that there are no shortcuts to moving forward through and beyond grief. For healthy grieving, you can't skip or bypass grief. So, your grief will be part of you as you travel. For most, with healthy grieving the burden of grief becomes more tolerable, and one builds the reliance and strength to carry this weight. We know by taking a slower but steady route we will encounter some of the important and beautiful lessons that loss has to teach us. Just as with the tortoise and the hare, taking the tortoise approach with hare-like bursts when we are lucky enough to have them, may be the best option. *Travel at your own pace.*

Truths from the Road: The Speed of Grief

"I feel like I'm walking in molasses up to my neck."

"Everything is stuck. I'm in slow motion and everyone has moved on."

Shift Happens! Do You Need to Downshift?

Prepare to stop. Are you encountering a need to slow down and possibly stop on your road to renewal following your loss? Sometimes shifting to a different gear may have the desired effect or pause to review where you currently are on this journey.

Solo or Solo Plus Travel?

Your road trip is YOURS. It is simply up to you how you want to travel and how to make that first step. For some it is important to work through grief by traveling solo. If you are having difficulty moving forward on your own, consider enlisting the support of a good friend to be your accountability partner. If no one is available, will you consider inviting God or a higher power to be at your side, *solo plus*?

Whether officially invited or not, your deceased loved one no doubt will be spiritually with you for at least parts of your journey. You are who you are in part because of this person, so acknowledge your loved one's spiritual presence, as you move forward on your own. It is comforting to know your loved one would be proud of the efforts you are making to create a new future for yourself.

If you are planning an actual physical rather than a metaphorical road trip, consider bringing a friend, a grandchild, or anyone who has the time and inclination to be a kind and understanding travel partner. A number of bereaved say they prefer to travel alone after their loss, while others look to a good friend or family member to accompany them. Or why not consider one trip by yourself, and another trip with one or more people involved as well.

Truths from the Road: Alone at Home

"Being alone, period."

"To see his empty chair about kills me."

Another said about her home, "I just sleep there, I don't live there."

"I seem to do very well when I am with people, and very badly when I am on my own."

"In the kitchen I pull down two plates, and it hits me."

"I can't return to a dark house. I need to leave all of the lights on."

Choose Your Road

There are many paths to the top of the mountain, but the view is always the same.

—Chinese proverb

You choose. Your road map can be a mixture of roads—for memory, for inspiration, for simply letting your mind unwind with the windows down and the wind in your face. Let your road map be a work in progress. You will be adjusting it as you go. The following are some of your road options.

HIGHWAY OF HOPE: Your constant and never changing road.

ASPIRATIONAL AVENUE: Visualizing your destination, *knowing* it is still in your future.

MEMORY LANE: Your tribute road, visiting places of remembrance and celebration.

SCENIC BYWAY: Slower but more beautiful, with time for reflection and gratitude.

UNMADE, UNPAVED, AND OFF ROAD: Perhaps this "less traveled" road can make for you "all the difference" in the words of the poet Robert Frost.

WILDERNESS PASS: The call of the wild, to get in touch within the wilderness of your grief, and get lost in your solitude.

Name Your Road Here:

_____

Truths from the Road: Traveling Solo

"Leave your loved one home," one man said. "I don't want to drag my deceased wife through the rest of my life."

"I am traveling alone cross country on my motorcycle to the Florida Keys to visit her. I scattered her ashes at the furthest most tip and I told her 'you'll have to swim from here.'"

One man stated, "I'm tough and I am just going to have to make it through on my own."

"I want my husband sitting next to me riding shotgun, as my co-pilot."

Map Designing: Your Life after Grief Road Map

An unpaved road keeps you from driving too fast, or forgetting too fast.
—Charles Kuralt

It is quite true what Philosophy says: that Life must be understood backwards. But that makes one forget the other saying: that it must be lived—forwards.
—Søren Kierkegaard

The best way out is always through.
—Robert Frost, "A Servant to Servants"

46

Your Hardest and Most Beautiful Unwanted Journey?

Please join me on what may be your hardest and most beautiful *unwanted* journey. Be on the lookout for those beautiful moments that will find you as you move forward through and beyond grief. A journey requires planning, preparation, and effort. Expect to travel through emotional regions of barren lands, desolate landscapes, treacherous mountain passes, and inclement weather, as well as fertile fields of abundance and cities of hope. I hope you will find beauty and inspiration along the way. Godspeed.

Truths from the Road: Your Hardest Journey?

"Losing my husband was a thousand times harder than I thought."

"My husband's death was like being hit up the side of my head with a baseball bat."

"I feel like my heart and soul was ripped out."

"A loss like mine takes you down to your hide."

"Life without her is much harder than I thought. It takes a lot more courage than I thought."

Design Your Own Road Map

All loss is unique, and your road map through and beyond grief will be uniquely yours. Since no road map has been written exactly for you, please join me to help create your own personalized road map. Remember, you will be traveling through both beautiful and desolate terrain. You are in charge. You have the right to press through rough terrain or push on through the challenges of steep climbs or hairpin turns. You may also think it is worthwhile to stop for a while, to enjoy a brief respite or work on challenges that are in front of you. This is your road map. I am delighted you are on board and committed to this road trip. *Welcome aboard!*

THE BEYOND GRIEF DESTINATION EQUATION: Your Formula for Reaching Your Destination

Doing + Being + Time = *Your Destination*
(Through and Beyond Loss and Grief)

What to Include in Your Road Map

Start with a blank road map. This is your *tabula rasa*, your clean slate. Visualize where you want to be in one year, two years, three years, and beyond to the end of your life. Remember you will have opportunities to adjust your road map as you travel forward.

- **Choose your destination.** Where do you want to go? Have you established an endpoint, a destination? Start with your ideal destination in mind.
- **Choose your time frame.** Have you established an ETA? Is it even possible to have a set ETA?
- **Choose to plan, plan, plan**
- **Choose your travel partner**
- **Choose your speed**
- **Choose your road**
- **How will I know which direction to go?** Listen to your internal GPS, your moral and spiritual compass will help lead you to your destination.

THE TOP 10 "ROAD TO RENEWAL" CHECKLIST

For best results, the following are the Top 10 areas to focus on to reach your destination of healthy healing and renewal after loss.

DOING—Daily is preferred. Increase dose when needed

1. Healthy self-care and wellness routine
2. Get out of the house, apartment, condo
3. Get out of your comfort zone
4. Remembrance—continuing relationship
5. Laughter

48

BEING—Daily is preferred.
Increase dose when needed

1. Hope
2. Trust
3. Gratitude
4. Forgiveness—yourself and others
5. Spiritual guidance—God or higher power

Journal Thoughts _____

_____

_____

_____

_____

_____

_____

_____

_____

_____

_____

_____

_____

_____

_____

_____

_____

_____

_____

_____

_____

_____

_____

_____

ROAD SCHOLAR ASSIGNMENT: Routine Road Map Maintenance

For best results, it is helpful to have a road map you can refer to and make regular additions and adjustments. It is satisfying to see progress, and to have a record of just how far you have traveled.

- **Daily Routine:** Take five—use your journal/daily appointment schedule once a day, spending no more than five minutes.

- **Weekly Check-in:** Take five—establish a time each week and take five minutes to review what you have planned for the upcoming week. Check for days with nothing planned and make plans to add structure to your week. Remember these plans can be super small.

- **Monthly Check-in:** Take five again, to look at the month ahead and write down possibilities that may interest you or activities you will have the ability and opportunity to do.

- **Revisit Road Map at Six Months:** Thirty-minute review—mark your calendar now, to revisit this book and your plan in six months. Send an encouragement/commitment letter to yourself. Write it and place in a drawer with the date to open it in 60 days (write the date on your calendar when to open it).

- **Revisit Road Map One Year Later:** Mark your calendar now, to revisit this book and your plan twelve months from today. Look back to see what you visualized for yourself, hit the reset button, and set your vision calendar, fine tuning adjustments, for the year ahead.

Part 2
DOING—
The Main Road

For the things that we have to learn before we can do them, we learn by doing them.
  —Aristotle, *The Nicomachean Ethics*

Life comes down to a simple choice: You're either busy dying, or busy living.
  —Frank Darabont, *The Shawshank Redemption*

I invite you to start something super-small today. Once you do something small, you will derive pleasure from the surprise and satisfaction of getting something done, especially after loss. This will motivate you to continue, thus over time help you move forward on your destination road. Be specific, and do a small concrete task. Act in the present rather than the future. The future will take care of itself. Create a spark, let it fly and illuminate your road ahead. DOING will be your Main Road to healing.

The Dos and Don'ts of Doing

THE DOs: This entire section is on the DOs of DOING. The dos in the following pages are strictly optional and completely a la carte, choose only those areas or ideas that appeal to you. *Try it and if you like it, keep at it, otherwise drop it.*

THE DON'TS: DON'T be overwhelmed by choice. Breeze through some of these suggested options and highlight areas you want to try now or revisit later. DON'T be held captive to a strict schedule or timeline. DON'T be hard on yourself if you are not able to do everything you want.

DOING DRIVE-THRU: The Four Steps

- **STEP 1: Believe**

  Step 1 is simply to *believe* that you will reach your destination beyond grief. Believing, when teamed with DOING and BEING, will be your important road markers on your road ahead. We all need something to *do*, something to look forward to, and we need someone to care about. Where do you want to first concentrate your energy, focus, and attention?

- **STEP 2: Begin with a Possibility List**

  Consider writing a Possibility List in your notebook including anything you may possibly want to do now or in the days and weeks ahead, plus things you think you would like to do in the more distant future. Write them down, and when you find yourself with some time and energy, pull out your Possibility List and take one out for a test drive.

- **STEP 3: Begin Your People-to-Contact List**

  In your notebook, begin compiling a People-to-Contact List that names people you may want to reach out and contact in the future when the spirit moves. Remember, this is a *potential* reconnect list, so putting a name on your list does not commit you to contacting that person at this time. Your list can contain old friends, high school friends, neighbors, family members, or business acquaintances with whom you have lost touch over the years. Naturally, many who have cared for a loved one put their lives on hold and personal relationships often have lapsed. When you are ready, let these people know you would like to reenter their lives to catch up and talk again. Be sure to include those contacts who live at a distance as well, as it is easier today to get in touch over the miles by telephone, email, or social media.

- **STEP 4: Remember The 50 Percent Rule**

  Grief is draining and saps our energy. Wise advice was given by the neighbor of a man I counsel for grief—she told him to "remember the 50 percent rule." She meant that after loss, expect only to be operating at half of your usual speed and capacity. Don't expect to be operating at peak or optimal performance, and even operating at 50 percent may be a stretch for many. In time, hopefully, you will return to your normal capabilities. Remember, there is no timetable or minimum speed limit for grief, and the last thing you need is an extra level of performance guilt, or one more thing in which to fall short. An important part of your healing is self-care and that means being gentle on yourself. Or, as the blues musician Willie Dixon wrote: "I'm built for comfort, I ain't built for speed." In our culture, faster is usually touted as better, and the faster and busier we are the better. Let's be sure to embrace the power and beauty of *slowness* and focus on living rather than speed. SLOW is one of those four-letter words that we need to embrace. Perhaps we need to set a LOW and SLOW bar for moving forward.

DOING: The Next Best Thing to BEING

- **DOING: Your Goldilocks Moment**

  DOING comes in all shapes and sizes, so choose one that is "just right" for you, "neither too hot nor too cold." This is a safe no-judgment zone, so whether you are considering small or large changes after your loss, think what is "just right" for you, and do it. Goldilocks would be proud!

- **DOING: Celebrate Small Steps**

  Baby steps, baby! Please be gentle with yourself and celebrate your little successes, the small steps on your Destination Road. You can begin anytime and anywhere you want. It doesn't truly matter what you do, as much as that you do something. Choose anything and do it now! Don't be overwhelmed by too many choices.

- **DOING: One a Day**

  Like the daily vitamin, try DOING once a day. For best results take one small step forward every day. One woman in her eighties told me in the days after her loss, "I don't have the energy to do everything at once, so I am scheduling one task or event each day, period." Wise advice.

- **DOING: The Snowball Effect**

  Start now with your baby steps. Your small actions have a greater impact than you would think. These small actions spur you on for further small actions, which over time compound. Your series of small actions culminates in a collective larger action and may lead to a significant change or personal milestone, which can be huge for you. Over time, DOING will seem more doable to you and may even seem natural and normal.

- **DOING: Just Carpe Diem It!**

  Harvest the day and leave as little as possible for tomorrow.

  —Horace, *Odes*

  This is a wonderful day. I've never seen this one before.

  —Maya Angelou

  The Latin phrase *carpe diem*, meaning "seize the day" is such a wonderful directive. Carpe diem can become a guiding principle for your new life ahead. Like a muscle, your call to action becomes stronger when called upon consistently over time. This spirit of action is the key ingredient of carpe diem which leads to a joy of living. This is hard to put into practice, but the effects are marvelous when put into motion. Nike's famous clarion call to action, "Just Do It" is the updated version of carpe diem and both phrases are common themes on change and motivation. No matter the spin, this ubiquitous call to action to improve your situation in life is appealing. If "seize the day" is too ambitious, why not seize the morning or the afternoon, or simply seize the moment? Grief is no different. We are already changed people as a result of significant loss. So, since we are already *changed* let's consider carrying this change into some positive territory, *for a change.*

- **DOING: Practice Makes Perfect**

  How do you seize the day when you don't feel like it? Fake it? I like to think *practice*, and I often advise practice, practice, practice. Even if you are not getting the desired benefit from the actions you initially try, keep with it. The more you practice doing, the more it will begin to feel satisfying to you. This is the reward of doing.

- **DOING AND GRIEF: The Odd Alliance**

  Is "doing" the antidote, the cure for grief? No, but doing can greatly help with a griever's frame of mind, if done in a positive and sensitive manner. You will need a clear understanding of when you need to put your foot on the accelerator to "do" and when you need to pump the brakes. You will also need to know when you simply need to shift into Neutral or Park. Sometimes you simply need to slow down, come to a full stop, and take a look back to be able to move forward.

- **DOING: Expect "Joy Lag"**

  Grief is like jet lag, expect some lingering effects after loss. At first, expect to go through the motions without feeling the benefit of joy. Think of this as a "joy lag" and even your "doing" today and in the near future may not produce the immediate results for which you were hoping. You may have to keep going through the motions for a while, without feeling the benefit, before joy and satisfaction finally begin to kick in. Sometimes, joy has to catch up!

- **DOING: Thinking Beyond Ourselves**

  If you don't want to do it for yourself, maybe you will need to do it for those you care about, both living and deceased. Be sure to enlist those important in your life to help in your personal reinvention.

- **DOING: What's Age Got to Do with It?**

  Age is not an excuse to stop growing. You are never too old to move forward with your grief and be a blessing to others, which in return will bless you. Sometimes I hear from grievers, "I'm too old" or "I guess I'm just set in my ways." Don't let your age matter. Many grievers I work with at advancing years are energized and have a sense of urgency as they know their time on Earth is no longer unlimited. One man told me, "I know I have five good years left and I want to make them count." One woman is in her eighties and is taking creative writing classes and studying French in readiness for her first trip to France. Another man, after loss at age ninety, formed a bell choir at his independent living center despite his limited hearing and it is one of the most popular activities offered there.

- **DOING: It's Never Too Late**

  No matter your age or circumstances, it is never too late to be open to new opportunities, no matter how small or large. After many years, now is the time to consider rekindling a past friendship that has lapsed. Perhaps it is time to revisit a past hobby, passion, or interest from your childhood or youth. Consider picking up your old saxophone to play again, start playing the piano once again, get out your trusty fishing pole, or revisit drawing or painting. Skill and performance are not important.

- **DOING: Your Wake-up Call**

  When loss or death visit us intimately, we are shaken to our core and it changes us. We have been on the receiving end of the proverbial wake-up call. This is good, it teaches us that life is short and precious. We are not on this earth forever, so we need to take full advantage of our circumstances, no matter how imperfect they may seem right now. If life is short, what can we do today to seize opportunities around us?

- **DOING Is Movement**

  I repeat, DOING IS MOVEMENT. Move even if you are not sure where to move, the rest will fall into place. The theme of this book is to *keep moving*, even when you don't feel like it. With small movements, comes MOMENTUM followed by MOTIVATION. Once you are motivated, you will begin to take additional steps of DOING that seem more natural and rewarding. Your confidence will grow and, hopefully, you will believe you are on your Destination Road. For any task that looks overwhelming, break it into smaller pieces, and know that it is a *process*, not meant to be completed all at once. Just keep moving. Will Rogers reminds us: "Even if you're on the right track, you'll get run over if you just sit there."

- **DOING: Nurture Serendipity**

  Serendipity will take you beyond the currents of what is familiar. Invite it. Watch for it. Allow it.
  —Jeanne McElvaney

  It's a bizarre but wonderful feeling, to arrive dead center of a target you didn't even know you were aiming for.
  —Lois McMaster Bujold

  Serendipity is not the product of patience; it's the product of action.
  —Audrey Moralez

Step out in faith, expect something good. I love the word *serendipity*. It is so light and playful. Serendipity is a word coined in the eighteenth century, that means finding something good without looking for it. When you move forward, you will find that the road you are on will lead you to another surprising and unexpected road. Serendipity will provide a smile to your face and help inject joy and contentment into your life.

56

Truths from the Road: What's your secret to coping with grief?

"I have the 3 Fs, my faith, my family, and my friends to get me through it."

"The cancer took him away and my anger was like a cancer too. I decided I was done with it, it was not going to do my any good, so I let it go."

"Life is exceptional," one man reported "of all things, a woman has come into my life that honors everything my late wife stood for."

"Believing and trusting in God, leaning on my family."

ROAD SCHOLAR ASSIGNMENT: "For the Road" Quotes

Why not copy one of the quotes from notable authors or ordinary grievers in this book? Write on an index card or sticky note a "for the road" quote that resonates with you. You can carry it in your purse, wallet, checkbook . . . where it will be seen and reinforced. You can give or share this quote with another person, which can be helpful in jump-starting a conversation.

Doing Begins with Structure: The Joy of Your Daily Routine

Build daily structure into your life. Simple daily routines give your day and week some well-needed structure. Daily routines can be both comforting and therapeutic and can offer a welcome sense of normalcy, when nothing seems normal. The challenge is filling in large gaps of time which are now present in your life after your loss. The best place to start is a daily routine of tasks to set the structural framework for the day and week ahead.

Control What You Can First

After loss it seems we have no control over anything. We do have or can have control over our daily and weekly routines. As one woman told me, "You just have to keep truckin'." Part of *truckin'* is developing a daily routine and sticking with it.

The Pros and Cons of Routine

Since each journey after loss is unique, take time to discover what it best for you. A structured daily routine gives grievers something constant in a changed world. Grievers report that having a routine can help reduce stress or anxiety by having some expected boundaries in their boundaryless world. On the other hand, others report that it is liberating to be free of routine. It is common for those who lived in a highly structured household with an early to bed/early riser mindset to enjoy the lack of a rigid schedule in the early weeks after loss. The decision is solely yours, but be careful to avoid a complete lack of routine with no boundaries. This can lead to a downward spiral depression loop if you stay up all hours of the night mindlessly watching television or scanning social media. Others report feeling guilty for letting previously set routines and standards in the house go by the wayside.

You decide what works best for you. Keep an open mind and adjust your daily routine (or lack of routine) as you move forward. Some minimal structure or routine is usually desired, but a strict adherence to routine can rob you of your opportunity for creativity and personal growth. Remember as you move forward your response to routine, structure, and life will change.

Starting Your Day: The Power of Good Morning Routines

You will want to be intentional to seek and develop ways to make your mornings set the tone for the rest of your day. Be sure to add some calm and reflection into your morning routine. Spiritual practice can be seen in the discipline of routine. Simple tasks, such as making the bed and putting dishes away, can be helpful to your mindset. You may want to create a structured time for a morning walk or exercise. Mix this in with some intentional time to reflect on your loved one or prayer or mediation. Build into your routine simple pleasures to include your favorite hot beverage, a special

treat, inspirational reading, and flowers to uplift your spirits. Include your daily routine from before your loss, taking care to adjust and structure it to best serve you.

The Morning Ritual: Give Yourself a Perk-up

As the nostalgic jingle states "the best part of waking up" is having a cup of Folgers coffee. Arranging a morning ritual makes it easier to greet the day. Carpe diem, seize the day with a treat, special tea or coffee, a morning ritual that puts a smile on your face.

MILEPOST TIP: Notable Quote

Take one of the quotes in this book and sit with it for a few minutes. Why did this quote catch your attention? How might you apply it today?

Daily Reflection: Prayer and Meditation

Daily reflection is the one area of DOING where you are working on your internal being as well. Only by stopping for a moment to be still and reflect are we able to see where we are and where we are going. (More on prayer and meditation is covered in the section on BEING.)

Ending Your Day: The Importance of a Good Nighttime Routine

Evenings and nights are often identified as "the hardest times" after a loss. For some it is the time that two people would come together after the day, for others it the time that errands and tasks are completed. Plan to create some good nighttime routines to cope.

- Set a specific time to go to bed, otherwise you may spiral out of control by staying up all night.

- Set a time to express gratitude for the day. Find one thing to be grateful for.

- Set a time before bed to pray or to "talk to" your loved one.

Weekend Strategy: Fast-forward the Weekend?

Planning for the weekend takes on a new meaning after a significant loss. In our non-grief filled existence and in the workforce, it is common to long for the weekend. TGIF! In grief, weekends may be tough. For many people Sundays are the worst. Many grievers try to fast-forward through the weekend because Mondays seem more normal—people are working, there are fewer gatherings with family and friends, or couples, and coping seems a little more manageable. When you recognize this, revise your weekend strategy to help you cope with the potential speed bumps that weekends bring.

- **CREATE A WEEKEND PLAN:** Begin working on your next weekend plan the weekend before. Take or make time over the week to reach out to old friends, reestablish previous contacts, and add new interests to your weekend calendar.

- **SATURDAY PLAN/SUNDAY PLAN:** Revise your daily routine structure to include at least one additional item on weekends. Know in advance what that will be.

Weekly Strategy: What to Do Weekly

- **GO AHEAD, YOU'RE WORTH IT: TREAT YOURSELF**

  Plan something extra special or even extravagant for yourself. If you like ice cream, if you like chocolate, whatever it is that is a treat for you, circle one day each week to make this happen.

- **LIKE REWARD POINTS? REWARD YOURSELF**

  Need motivation? Award reward points to yourself or enjoy a little treat as a reward for completing a task that had been nagging you. Accomplishing a small task gives a sense of well-being and encourages you to do more. *Keep the positive rewards or treats coming!*

- **DO NOTHING**

  Plan a "do nothing" session each week. To do this, you will need to unplug and to get off the grid for a few hours or a full day. The Dutch call it *niksen* which is the art of doing nothing. This is harder than it sounds, but try to avoid all screens, your smart phone, computer, or television during the allotted time period. As a result of being idle, your engine continues to run but you are simply in park or neutral. Perhaps this will be an enforced inner expedition of yourself.

Journal Thoughts _____

_____

_____

_____

_____

_____

Get in the routine each week, to review your weekly calendar. Try to make sure that you have added something to do or someone to contact each day. I suggest doing this at the beginning or end of each week. This should provide *encouragement,* not judgment. If an item on your agenda is not accomplished, no big deal, push the item to the following week. *Plan your work, work your plan.*

MILEPOST TIPS: On a Quest

Consider adding any of the following to your journey.

Quest to Invest

Consider it all an investment in your new future. To best invest in yourself, you will notice that your efforts will include others, and that will give your quest meaning and give your life purpose. Your life is worth it, you owe it to your loved one, friends, and family to continue living, even though its hard. Strive to make the most of your days ahead.

Quest to Be Interested in Life

Chicken and egg. Which came first?: INTERESTED IN LIFE or an INTERESTING LIFE? Perhaps to be interested in life again, you need to begin *doing*, trying anything possible, looking for that elusive spark. It is DOING that gets you on the road to recovery and finding your new direction. We know life is short, we know that to take advantage of opportunities, we need to keep moving. Keep moving forward. *Life goes on.*

Quest to Build Self-Confidence

Every small step, every baby step builds confidence. This extra confidence builds on itself, it gives you the added confidence to reach out for help from others, to join groups, to start things, to further believe in—and expand—your "I can" mentality. This gives you the confidence to tackle your fears or obstacles and allows you to grow little by little.

Quest to Make Mile Markers
Your Daily Friend

As you travel on this journey, you will notice just how slowly the mile markers on the road go by. Make these DAILY mile markers your friend, showing that you have made progress. First you survived today, then you survived another day, and soon you will move from surviving to LIVING AGAIN.

Ideas and Strategies for Doing: In and Outside Your Home

The best things in life are often waiting for you at the exit ramp of your comfort zone.

—Karen Salmansohn

Inject New Routines at Home

- **READIN', 'RITIN', and 'RITHMATIC**

  o **Read, Read, Read:** Find inspirational and helpful books and blogs on loss and grief to help with your processing. Good ideas are everywhere. Keep your eyes open for any reading that can help propel you down your healing road.

  o **Write On! Consider Journaling:** Consider the power of journaling, it has the power to transform. Keep a daily journal. If you do not think you have anything to say, simply write: "Here I am, I got up this morning and I decided to write in my journal. I can't think of anything to write." Then you could write something like, "I never thought I would write in a journal. I guess I am doing this because maybe it will help me." Be honest and write what comes naturally. Over time your journal will start to look like part diary, part confessional, and part aspirations for the future. You will be surprised when you look back several months or a year later just how far you have come in your thinking, healing, and finding a new direction in life. Once you commit to writing in a journal you will be in tune with your spiritual and inner self, which is a beautiful thing.

ROAD SCHOLAR ASSIGNMENT: On the Road Daily Journal

Create your own or obtain a journal that allows for 365 entries to complete in one year. Complete daily a five-minute or less entry. Simply write a thought, even just *HELLO*, or something you might want to do or look into in the year ahead. Separate each day with the top portion to record your emotions, thoughts, and dreams, followed by the bottom part indicating something you would like to do or someone to contact in the near future or more distant future. Date each entry, so looking back you see your progress on your Beyond Grief Journey.

- **ADDING UP: Do You Know Your Numbers?**

  Do you know where you stand financially after your loss? If the task of paying bills or taking care of finances falls to you for the first time, make sure you receive help with your financial numbers and any related paper-work. Loss is all about change, and finances can be a big part of the equation. Make it your business to be aware of any changes your loss brings to you. Sometimes we worry more about that which is not out in the open. Money is not always an easy topic to look at, but knowing your numbers can provide peace-of-mind to you for the future.

- **ORDER AND CLEANLINESS: Controlling What Can Be Controlled**
  - **Consider a Mental Health Declutter Session**
    When you have an energy burst, consider a twenty-minute declutter session in your home. It will help with your mental outlook and give you a baby step sense of accomplishment. Start with something simple, clear out a drawer, a closet, or half of a closet.
  - **High on Hygiene?**
    You may decide to opt for hygiene, rather than "low-giene." By keeping your surroundings clean, you may feel in control of at least one thing in your life. One man after his loss reported: "I never have dirty dishes in the sink." Another man admitted, "I learned right away that I would need to learn to iron, and now I iron everything."

- **INJECT NEW ROUTINES OUTSIDE THE HOME**
  - **"Get Outta" the House, Leave Your House Daily:** If you are retired or not working, run errands every day to get you out of the house. With additional time on your hands from your loss, you are not always looking for maximizing time efficiency, so stretch out errands and appointments. Have something each day that gets you out of the house.
  - **Shop/Browse Daily:** Find a reason to go to the grocery store, drug store, or hardware store daily as a healing strategy. Browse or shop, this gets you out of the house, which helps stimulate the *healing agent* in your recovery from loss.
  - **Why Not Take a Daily Cruise:** If you drive, why not drive around a lake or pond, or a site of natural beauty? Explore areas you never have been before or return to nostalgic scenes with a new and healing perspective.
  - **Change It Up at Work:** Work can be your friend after loss. You will already have a built-in agenda for each day you work. Why not take advantage of any offers to meet with coworkers for lunch or after hours? If you have the energy, plan a stop before or after work for something of interest or pleasure.
  - **Going Public:** Be in public places. Start with becoming comfortable being in public places where it is perfectly normal to be without a

companion. Over time you may find yourself building up confidence to go to places alone where many people may be with a companion but certainly some will be alone.

- **FIND A NEW PUBLIC HANGOUT**
  - o **Coffee or Sandwich Shop:** Coffee shops and sandwich shops are full of people on their own, who bring a book, magazine or newspaper, or laptop to work quietly in a public place. There is no stigma in this as a large number of people are purposely there on their own.
  - o **Library or Bookstore:** You will get a double bonus: to read and learn new ideas while at the same time getting you out of the house and into the public arena. You will find it perfectly acceptable to be alone and on your own as virtually everyone else will be too. While you are there, check out library book clubs or author's events.

- **MAKE A DATE WITH YOURSELF**
  If you don't have someone to go with you to a movie, concert, or sporting event, consider going on your own. If you're self-conscious about seeing people you know, go to a movie or restaurant in a different part of the city where you will be unknown. Many people embrace singleness and attend events solo. Feel free to join the trend.

- **FIND A NEW GROUP TO JOIN**
  - o **Join a Bridge Club:** Learn to play bridge and join a local bridge group or online bridge club. Check online or at your community center or library for groups that are getting underway. Playing bridge or other card games helps sharpen your mind and gets you involved with others in the community.
  - o **Join a Book Club:** Community Centers, libraries, places of worship, and bookstores all have book clubs as do many neighborhood associations. Consider joining one. You might want to try a reading genre that is completely new to you.
  - o **Join a Movement Group:** Physical movement plus being with others is a double bonus. Perhaps yoga, Pilates, tai chi, or another exercise group is right for you. Consider a walking group that exercises in a mall or community center.
  - o **Join a Support Group:** This is strongly recommended. Research a good support group in your area to join. The power of being with people and in community, especially after a loss, is huge.
  - o **Find Your Local Community Center:** Community centers have most of the above activities and more. Some even serve lunch.

SCENIC OVERLOOK:
Where do you see yourself
one year from today?

Asked that question, one woman answered: "Doing what I do today. I am in a good spot right now. I enjoy my solitude. When I want to be more sociable, I invite friends over. When I need 'centering' I come to this support group."

- **LEARN A NEW SKILL: Find a New Hobby**

  Take a class, learn a new skill, allocate what time and resources you have to invest in yourself. Do not expect to find the perfect opportunity, find the best fit for you and try it on for size.

  o Learn to sew, play the piano, or study a foreign language. Take a class or workshop on cooking, jewelry making, woodworking, or genealogy to cite a few examples.

Truths from the Road: How do you see yourself one year from now?

"I am in a good place now. I see myself doing the same thing one year from now, continuing to care for my cat and making sure she has her medications. Maybe a little more social, inviting others to my house."

- **DEVELOP A NEW SOCIAL STRATEGY: Joining and Inviting**
  o **Be Open to Accepting Invitations:** Decide to be open to accepting invitations, even if you are only half inspired. If helpful, plan to stay only a short time, arrive late and leave early.

  o **Be Open to Inviting Others:** In time, make it a goal to invite others to join you in interests you have or want to pursue.

  o **Be a "Suggester":** Make suggestions for coffee, lunch, or a drop-in visit to friends. For many people, being a suggester does not come easy. That's OK, take your time and trust that you have the ability and right to become a suggester.

- o **Standing Dates:** Standing dates are awesome. Is there a friend you can go with on a regularly scheduled walk, say every Wednesday morning? Or a friend you can meet weekly for coffee? Consider joining community organizations that have scheduled weekly or monthly meetings.

- o **Pick Up the Phone:** Plan to pick up the phone and get in touch. Plan to call certain friends in the evenings or weekends or whenever you feel lonely. Set up phone appointments, for specific times or as needed. Add another contact or two from your past to reconnect with. This works great for long-distance friends. **Evening friend phone calls:** Identify two or more friends or family whom you can call in the evenings on a regular basis. **Weekend friend phone calls:** Identify two or more friends or family whom you can call on the weekend as well.

SELF-CARE: Wellness Starts with Good Self-care

EAT, SLEEP, MOVEMENT: The Foundation Blocks of Self-care

For this section on DOING, we will focus on the three foundation blocks of self-care wellness: Eat, Sleep, and Movement. Without these three foundation blocks for self-care, our Destination Road will be nearly impassable. In the section on BEING, we will examine strategies for *internal* self-care wellness.

After a loss, it is so easy to get out of kilter in every aspect of life. You will need to take great care of yourself. Many grievers have neglected their own health to look after a loved one. We are no good to others or to ourselves if we do not practice good self-care wellness. Particularly, as we age, we need to pay more attention to our personal maintenance, and once entering middle age and beyond "it's all maintenance, maintenance, maintenance." After the loss of a go-to person in your life, you will need an extra dose of self-care maintenance. Self-care is not selfish, it is self-kindness. Please plan to build self-care into the margins of your life.

EAT: Eat to Live

Grief can play havoc on eating habits. A lot of times, grievers see large fluctuations in their weight, either losing their appetite or gaining extra pounds with the added stress of change, worry and grief. Good self-care means developing healthy eating and nutrition habits. The usual challenges for grievers are: learning to buy groceries for one, learning to cook for one, and learning the importance of eating properly.

SLEEP: Sleep Hygiene

Grief can be very disruptive to sleep and we need our sleep. Many have difficulty going to sleep, staying asleep, or getting back to sleep after waking up in the middle of the night or several times in the night. Explore these suggestions for healthy sleep hygiene:

- Establish a standard bedtime and stick with it.

- Avoid caffeine and eating, physical activity and exercise, and stimulus from electronic screens before bedtime.

- Ensure your sleep area is free of reminders of work or unfinished projects and clutter.

- Mute your cell phone.

- Avoid checking the clock or phone every time you wake up.

- You may consider investing in a white noise machine to block out any outside noise.

- If you have lost your sleeping partner, perhaps you may want to sleep in the middle of the bed, or you may want to curl up with a large pillow for comfort.

- You may want to practice relaxation techniques, such as prayer, deep breathing, and meditation, or simply count your blessings until you fall asleep.

- There are numerous natural sleep aids on the market that may work for you, such as chamomile tea or a melatonin natural supplement to help you fall asleep.

MOVEMENT: Move to Exercise

Physical movement and exercise are vital to your health and wellness. The bottom line: *keep moving* and include exercise in your daily or weekly routine. Simple exercise routines for all levels in the home are readily available online and in bookstores.

- **MOVEMENT:** Make a conscious effort to make movement part of your daily routine. The more you are physically active in and outside your home, the better mental outlook you will have. Try adding physical chores or projects at home as you are able. If a task is too involved, try stretching out your efforts over several sessions.

- **WALKING THERAPY:** Try to add a ten-minute walk to your daily routine either by yourself or with a friend or neighbor. The physical benefits of walking are widely reported to help elevate emotional well-being. Solo walks are highly recommended after loss and are therapeutic. One man decided it was very important to him after his loss to take solo walks every morning: "I talk to my wife and let her know what is going on in my life. I'm sure people think I must be some nut walking and talking to myself."

OTHER FORMS OF SELF-CARE TO PRACTICE

Self-care is a 360-degree view of yourself, it is absolutely holistic, taking care of your entire being, the emotional, physical, and spiritual sides of yourself.

- Pamper your soul. Begin the day with reflection, such as prayer, mindful relaxation, or meditation.

- Practice gratitude daily, consider a one-minute daily offering of gratitude.

- Build in daily a joy or happiness break. Practice anything that puts a smile on your face and song in your heart.

- Journal writing is self-care for the soul and brain.

- Money care, healthy boundaries, routine wellness and screening exams, and decluttering are all self-care, as they can help relieve stress in your life.

PAUSE BUTTON
Time for a Self-Care Check

How beautiful it is to do nothing, and then rest afterward.
—Spanish proverb

Take a deep breath and be honest with yourself. If reading this book is making you feel more anxious or overwhelmed, then you have permission to take a leave of absence, for a day, week, or month. Hit the pause button and enjoy your mini sabbatical; we will welcome you back. This road map is for you. Do what works best for you, and work at your own pace.

Truths from the Road: Pause Button

One bereaved man shared the following insight, "Sometimes we can find ourselves at a dead end and exhausted. In bereavement one can become frenetic with action to keep pain and sadness at bay. In bereavement we can become stuck, self-indulgent, narcissistic, in owning and clinging to our loss and pain. When we find ourselves at these dead ends, it's OK just to pause, breath, acknowledge that we needed to pursue that dead end at that time: nothing lost; you still have all your future in front of you."

DOING: Coping Strategies to Consider after Your Loss

What should I expect from others?

Unfortunately, after loss we may need to gear down our expectations of others. We live in a hurry-up culture that is averse to death. Our society is not skilled at supporting grievers. Even well-meaning people struggle with someone grieving because they are often ill-equipped to cope.

- **LOOK FOR SUPPORT IN UNEXPECTED PLACES**

  Be open to receive a supportive ear, a supportive shoulder, or simply someone with a compassionate heart. Even if you think you have absolutely nothing in common with this individual, because of age, background, or life experiences, keep an open mind and be prepared to allow an unexpected person to be blessed by helping you.

- **WHAT DO I TELL OTHERS?**

  Tell your story about your loved one as often as you can. Weave the name of your loved one into this story. Storytelling normalizes your relationship with your loss. In our support group, we always grant our guests

69

the opportunity to briefly tell about their loved ones. It is absolutely vital for your healing to have a safe place or opportunity for telling your story.

- **WHAT DO I TELL PEOPLE WHEN THEY ASK HOW I AM DO-ING?**

  If it is someone you care about and who is prepared to listen, tell them how you are really feeling. If it is someone who is asking to be polite, then a stock answer will suffice, such as, "I'm fine," "I'm doing OK," or "I have my ups and downs and thank you for asking."

- **WHAT DO I TELL PEOPLE WHO DO NOT KNOW ABOUT MY LOSS?**

  People you have not seen for some time, people you recently met, and other acquaintances may not know about your loss. You might bring it up or they might unknowingly ask about your loved one thinking he or she is still alive. Expect this to happen, even a year or more after your loss. When this happens, consider it an opportunity for you to move forward on your road to healing.

- **GET THE WORD OUT**

  Start spreading the news. Tell others what you are doing, learning, and what you are considering for the future. Small details count! Many after a tough loss seem more eager to share their recent experiences and plans for the future. Keep spreading the news.

- **ASK FOR HELP? ASK FOR DIRECTIONS?**

  The standard joke that "men don't ask for directions" seems appropriate here. If we do not lower our pride to ask for directions, how can we ask for help for matters of the heart? You probably have a network of people who are willing to help. Sometimes this network is a little weak or is rusty or has not been recently nurtured or cultivated, but nonetheless it is still there. Call on this group. People want to help people when they can.

  HOW TO ASK FOR HELP: Ask: "Would you please be able to help with a question I have?" If the answer is yes, proceed: "What would you do in my situation?" Their answer is not telling you what to do, but rather telling you what they would do—or what they think they would do-—in your situation. There is a difference. You can let this person know that you plan to ask others for their advice as well. Thank them for any advice given and then decide which direction is best for yourself.

- **THE IMPORTANCE OF STOCK ANSWERS TO DEFLECT CURI-OSITY SEEKERS**

  You will be asked: "What are you going to do now?" Ideally, by doing the exercises in this book, you will have a few ready-made answers to tell

70

others. Your road map is your frame of reference. Hopefully you can share two or three anchor points of what you have planned for the year ahead, such as "I will be visiting my sister who lives in California," "I am planning to clear out the basement and have a garage sale," or "I have signed up for classes to learn to play the guitar, something I've always wanted to do."

KEEP YOUR POWDER DRY: No need to reveal your inner thoughts to the casual observer; rather, save this for your go-to people that are in your corner, those who have earned your trust.

DOING: Coping as a Single Person in a Couples' World

- **SO NOW I AM SINGLE**

   This may be the first time for you to be living alone since you left home as a young adult. Finding yourself single after many years may seem like being exiled to a desolate foreign island. When singleness is sudden, rather than by choice, the change can seem cruel. One man expressed how hard it was to sign legal papers after the death of his wife: "It was the first time in forty-seven years that I had to sign my name with the box marked 'Single'—that really hit me like a ton of bricks." Being single seems to strip away those unspoken perks that come with being a couple. Many newly single people tell me they now have a sense of being demoted, feeling for the first time like second-class citizens. Prime time—evenings, weekends, and holidays—seem to be reserved for couples, while being single you may find yourself being relegated to the daytime coffee and lunch slots for get-togethers with those from your former couples' world.

- **LEARNING NEW COPING SKILLS IN A COUPLES' WORLD**

   Grievers over time have adjusted and found activities they can do as a single person. These are activities that they thought they would never be able to do by themselves. After a number of months, one woman is now attending concerts and movies on her own, something she earlier had said would not be possible. Another person goes back to her favorite Chinese restaurant that she and her husband used to frequent and whose owner they knew. "I just bring a book, enjoy great food, and feel comfortable being on my own, in a comforting place." Another woman goes out to breakfast three times a week to places where she and her husband ate breakfast every morning: "I bring my memory book with me from the funeral which has photos and memories of my husband to show to people that ask about him. I feel comforted going to these places because he is with me."

• CRASHING THE COUPLES' WORLD

The good news is that people today are becoming more aware of loss and the importance to reach out to those who have lost a partner. There is slow progress in this area, and I encourage you to consider attending couples' events in the future. Be sure you are comfortable with those attending. Be, and you *can* be, selective about which event you decide to attend. You may want to plan to arrive late and leave early. If you are not up for joining the couples' group at first, politely decline and express thanks for the invite, and ask that they think of you next time. *Remember you were an important contributor before your loss, and you will continue to be in the future.*

MILEPOST TIP: Inviting Couples?

Invite one member of a couple, or the couple to join you. Even in a couples' world, couples don't have to do everything together. Retired couples need some space from their partners freeing up opportunity for you. Invite a friend to a concert, lecture, play, or sporting event, in which you know the other half of the couple would have no interest. Or, if you can afford it, consider purchasing three tickets or three season tickets, one for yourself and two for a couple as your treat. The tickets can be free or a small investment to help you on the road to finding your "new" you.

LET IT BE: Letting Go and Letting In

In the process of letting go you will lose many things from the past, but you will find yourself.
—Deepak Chopra

We must be willing to let go of the life we have planned so as to have the one that is waiting for us.
—Joseph Campbell

There is love in holding and there is love in letting go.
—Elizabeth Berg

Sometimes the hardest part isn't letting go but rather learning to start over.
—Nicole Sobon

LETTING GO: The Stuff

Grievers tell me that it can be easier to let go of some of the physical stuff than to let go of some of the emotional stuff, such as guilt, anger, and regret. The emotional stuff will be addressed in the next section on BEING.

- **IS MOVING FORWARD LETTING GO?**

Yes and no. Let me explain.

Yes, moving forward is letting go of the false concept that "I am not worthy" or "I don't deserve to be happy again."

No, moving forward is never forgetting or letting go of the memories or impact your loved one *has* on you.

EPIPHANY ALERT: Today Is the Day!

Leap and the net will appear.

—John Burroughs

Leap Day. Decide that *today is the day* to take one leap. The leap can be small. It can even be an IOU agreement to yourself to take this leap the first moment you have energy. Remember grief drains our energy. If you can't *do* it now, write it down on your Opportunity/Possibility List to claim when your energy returns. You probably know people who woke up one morning with a resolve to do something difficult, and they did it. You, too, can claim *today is the day* to take a leap.

LETTING GO: Possessions

Possessions, possessions, possessions. It is a challenge to know what to do with the physical possessions of your loved one. From closets to basements, from workrooms to garages, items that no longer have a use for you need to be addressed over time. You may wonder, how soon is too soon for me to dispose of these possessions? For some who are grieving, the disposal of possessions is another opportunity to be judged on their mourning. Grievers report being scrutinized at the speed or lack of speed in which they shed their loved one's possessions. Move at your own pace. It is not uncommon to hear grievers say in retrospect that they wished they had taken their time to dispose of these possessions, rather than heading to the landfill. It is heartwarming to hear of the loving care that many grievers take to find a good and appropriate home for those no longer needed items. Possessions are memories and their careful handling is part of the healing process. If you have large or valued collections, you will probably need additional time, help, and assistance, even an appraisal.

LETTING GO: The House

Should I stay or should I go?

—Joe Strummer and Mick Jones of The Clash

Grievers are often asked, even as early as the funeral: "What are you going to do with the house?" Loss seems to trigger an avalanche of additional assumed changes, including giving up a principal residence or vacation home. Sometimes due to finances or practicality, it may no longer be feasible to remain in your home. If this happens, you will experience a secondary loss—saying goodbye to memories, favorite nooks and crannies, and the comfort of familiarity. Perhaps you will want to give thanks for this house, and what it meant to your life, and the life you shared. Letting go, done right, can be cathartic and freeing of some underlying obligations, responsibilities, expenses, and physical and financial upkeep.

MILEPOST TIP: Claim Your One-year Free Pass

You probably have heard the well-known saying, "Don't make any major decisions in the first year after your loss." I fully recommend that you weigh this time-tested adage and adopt it if it is your choice and to YOUR ADVANTAGE. Many feel some degree of pressure to make decisions which are not always in their best interest. When asked what you are planning to do about "the house" or any other major issue, the best answer is to play the "Adage Advantage Card." Let everyone know you are cashing in your one-year free pass. This decision is *perfectly fine* and *perfectly normal.* When you are uncertain, the best answer is to kick that question down the road until you are ready to answer it. For others who have been waiting to make changes, often for several years with an ailing loved one, then you have the green light to act as soon as you are ready. Remember: You are in charge of your life. Bottom line: Use it to your advantage.

LETTING GO: Clearing Out Your Parents' House

The tasks and duties of loss, where paperwork and hard work intersect. One man tasked with clearing out his parents' house asked, "How do I liquidate sixty-two years of memories? I have to liquidate someone's entire life. No, I have to liquidate two people's entire lives." Another woman tasked with closing her parents' estate said, "Driving by my parents' house with new owners in it was easier than closing their trust with their names on the pages." Siblings and other family members are often at odds on the pace of this process as well as the level of sentimentality in the process of letting go. If you are overwhelmed and can afford it, you may want to push out the timetable for getting this done.

- **MEMENTOS AND VISUAL REMEMBRANCES**

  Everyone is different. After loss some continue to have photos and mementos of their loved one prominently displayed, while others remove them. Others have said they have brought even more mementos into full view. One woman stated, "I want to keep everything, but I want to change the location of prominence of some of the mementos and photo frames." Some want more visual reminders, as it is comforting to them, and some want less. One man told me he had to move out of his house into an apartment, as the "memories were just too powerful" in the house. It is common for many to have a special spot for remembrance and a place where they can say goodbye and hello upon exiting and entering the house.

- **THE ANSWERING MACHINE**

  For those with phone landlines, the decision has to be made whether to keep or erase the answering machine message. Many do not erase the message as this may be one of the few samples of their loved one's voice. Others, for security purposes, may prefer the message announcement that a couple is living at this residence. Some will continue to keep a loved one's cell phone for the messages and not close out social media accounts.

- **THE RING? TO WEAR OR NOT TO WEAR?**

  At some point you may reach a time when you will consider what to do with your wedding ring or another remembrance ring from your loved one. When do you decide to stop wearing the wedding ring? This can be an emotional decision, as it is yet one more reminder of symbolically distancing yourself from your loved one. Some will place the ring on a necklace, rather than the finger. A woman told me "I take it off, not to forget, but as a reminder that I am moving forward. I will put it on for protection, or to send a signal that there is someone in my life." The decision to remove a wedding ring can be a powerful milestone on your destination road to renewal.

LETTING IN

The two important areas of "letting in" to the new life you are creating are: PEOPLE and NEW EXPERIENCES. One bereaved woman had this advice: "I always say 'PLUS'." I always add plus to anything I come across in life. The plus is the blessing." Plus living starts with letting in. You have experienced the *minus* with your loss, now moving forward, I invite you to move into *plus* living by adding new experiences and relationships into your life.

LET PEOPLE IN

People who need people are the luckiest people in the world.
—Appice, Stein, Bogert, and Martell "People"

For it won't be long 'til I'm gonna need somebody to lean on
—Bill Withers, "Lean On Me"

THE POWER OF PEOPLE. John Donne once said, "No man [or woman] is an island." The myth of independence, that a person needs no one, is just a myth. We need each other. Ask for help, people are ready to help. Learn to "let people in" again. One man who is grieving the loss of his son concluded "Life is a team sport." You will need at least one person to lean on, and preferably several people, on your journey ahead. This may not be easy for you, but it is well worth the effort. Trust that the right people, not necessarily those you have imagined, will be there for you moving forward.

- **WHO WILL BE YOUR NEW GO-TO PERSON?**

  Who will be your "trip advisor" on your road trip?

  After significant loss, one of the greatest challenges is to find this new person or to promote another in your life to this role. Find your go-to person and while you are at it, why stop with one person, start assembling your go-to team.

- **YOUR GO-TO TEAM, WHO'S IN YOUR HUDDLE?**

  On your go-to team you may have people who are great to support you for one area of your life but not another. Why not mix and match these friends and family members so you have support in all areas of your life? Building your team means developing an ample pool from which to draw support and inspiration. By doing so, you do not overly burden or wear down one single friend or contact. You may find a friend that is available to you only in the daytime, another that would be more of a nighttime or weekend friend. You will also want to cultivate phone or social media friends as well. This will be your huddle, your support system moving forward.

- **PEOPLE POWER, FINDING YOUR ACCOUNTABILITY PARTNER**

  Identify and develop a friend or family member to walk alongside you on your journey. You do not need to share your inner thoughts and grief with everyone, but it is very therapeutic if you are able to confide in one or two trusted people. Ask this identified friend if he or she would be your accountability partner. This person will help build your resilience and keep you accountable and on your journey to your new future. You may be surprised which person is able to stand in the gap and make a difference in this particular chapter of your life. It is often the case that those people you were counting on were no-shows, not interested or equipped to walk alongside you at this time. Your accountability partner could also be mourning his or her own loss and on the road to discovering their new self as well.

MILESTONE TIP: Add Some Teflon to Your Person

Expect unhelpful comments and lack of understanding from individuals you encounter daily. Since we are all a little more fragile after loss, we can be hurt by well-meaning but insensitive comments. One woman recalled that she was incensed from the comments of a well-meaning friend: "I was really ticked off when a good friend of mine said 'Shouldn't you get some help for your depression.' I told her it's not depression, it's grief." The beauty of Teflon is that food does not stick when heated. When we get heated and upset it is easy for criticism or unkind comments, even when offered with good intentions, to get under our skin and to stick. The newly bereaved are particularly vulnerable with heightened sensitivity. Often those closest to us can really push our buttons. Coat an extra layer of Teflon on yourself, and let any unhelpful or hurtful comments roll off you in slick Teflon fashion.

- **FRIENDS: Go for the Gold and Silver Too**

  You probably know the well-known Girl Scout song: "Make new friends, but keep the old. One is silver, the other is gold." How do people make new friends? As we age, finding ways to make new friends becomes more difficult, especially if you had put your life on hold while caregiving. Perhaps we need to reframe the word "friends" to simply mean anyone with whom you can have a meaningful exchange. The bottomline is that you will have to get in the game again, which may mean taking a risk by making the first overture to start a new relationship. It can be as natural as meeting someone at the grocery store, striking up a conversation, and realizing you have something in common. You can say something as simple as "I would love to talk to you more, could we meet to have coffee or to go on a walk?" The best opportunities for making new friendships are through activities in which you are involved. Perhaps it will be in a class you join or at a place you volunteer. Start slowly and suggest something simple and see what happens. You have nothing to lose but a little pride.

- **HOW TO RECONNECT WITH OLD FRIENDS**

  Reconnecting with old friends is like riding a bicycle, it comes back easily. Pick up the phone, and be honest, that you have lost touch, that "life got in the way." With your loss you have something newsworthy to impart as well. You can say something such as: "When I lost _____, it really made me take stock of my life, and to be grateful for all those I have enjoyed being with in the past. I was thinking of you and I just wanted to call and say 'thank you' for being such a good friend when we were in school [or worked together, or whatever]." Friendships are a two-way street, but be the first to say: "I'm sorry I haven't been in touch." This is just a touch base call, no need to ask to get together at this point. If the phone call went well, then ask the follow-up question: "Is it alright if I call you sometime in the future? It's been great hearing your voice." When you ask for permission, with no commitment on the other person's part, it is easier to reconnect again in the near future.

- **WHERE ARE SUPPORTIVE PEOPLE?**

  Looking to be around like-minded supportive people? Try a support group. it is amazing how liberating it is to know that you are not the only one dealing with loss. Those who come to our support groups tell me that "it was a life saver" and they "could not have got through this" without it. Find a good support group in your area and give it a try.

Truths from the Road: Support Groups

"Great to know that there are others who think and feel the same way I do."

"I have no family. This group is my family."

"Thank you for this lifeline."

"Friends tell me that I am a completely different person having attended."

"There is comfort in knowing that I am not alone."

"I was surprised by the love that emanates in this group"

When Isolation or Lack of Mobility Is Not a Choice

You may be part of our population in which isolation or outward mobility is an issue. You may find it impossible or very difficult to leave the house because of your physical health, or you may live in an isolated location with limited access to people. Studies have shown that a greater number of people are living more isolated by choice and are not as engaged in the world as had been the case a generation ago. Although the grieving process is greatly helped by living in community, the opportunities to participate in a "virtual community" offer an alternative. I am hopeful that you will be able to connect with others in a meaningful way through any avenue that presents itself.

MILEPOST TIP: Are You People Challenged?

Grievers sometimes admit: "we have always lived isolated lives" or "we have never been social" or "I am not a social person or a group person." If you are "people challenged" that is perfectly fine. Knowing yourself is so important, and your healing road may be without the benefit of face-to-face human interaction. You, too, may be thinking, as one woman reported, "I know I should AND need to be around people, but I just can't." Then, relax, don't fret, whatever your comfort level with others is, remember you are *perfectly normal*, and that it is *absolutely natural* to think this way after loss.

People, Your "Emotional Insurance Policy"

You *do* have an "Emotional Insurance Policy" for your road trip, and that is *people*. Emotional fender bender? If struggling on this journey, it's time to cash in this policy. The "right" people may not be easily recognizable to you or easy to find, but there are people willing to help you. Raise your antenna to see who can be of help to you on your way.

Consider Letting in New Experiences

All the tips and suggestions in this DOING section are meant to give you some inspiration to test drive one or two that resonate with you. Grievers successfully *let in* new experiences, such as sharing in a support group or being able to put air in a car tire for the first time, reaching out to old friends, accepting invitations to go with couples to a movie or concert. Some grievers say that they have *let in* self-care, that they are now following up with their own health issues and addressing long-neglected health concerns. Others *let in* by beginning to plan for the future. *Letting in* goals, such as moving to a warmer climate for the winter or looking forward to a cruise on the Rhine next year, can become a welcome component of healthy healing.

Truths from the Road:
New and Continued Interests

"I opened up my guest house/bed and breakfast. It had been closed with my wife's health. I don't know why I did it, I don't need the money, I will do it for a while to see if I want to continue it."

- **LETTING IN: Consider Pet Adoption**

  Animals are such agreeable friends—they ask no questions, they pass no criticisms.
  —George Eliot

  A pet can be a true blessing on the road beyond grief. Consider adding to your life a cat or dog if you do not have one, or replacing a pet that has died. Professionals can advise you on the right type of pet for your living space and lifestyle. If you don't want to commit to long-term pet ownership, you might want to volunteer at an animal shelter.

- **LETTING IN: Team Up with a Friend or Colleague to Start a Home Business**

  What better way to get back on your feet than by getting your teeth into a project leading to a home business. If you have an interest and aptitude, consider producing artisan crafts or fresh food items and go green. Find a craft, product, or service that you can create or add value through personalization, such as monogramming. Start small, experiment first with friends and family, and when ready sell items at a local market or online.

- **LETTING IN: Adopt a Cause, Become a Volunteer**

  Adopt a cause that speaks to your heart and donate your time and energy. Become a volunteer, you will have an opportunity to meet people, be productive, and give meaning to your life. Try to volunteer during times in the evening or weekend that you feel most vulnerable in your grief.

- **LETTING IN: Sign Up for Season Tickets and Subscriptions**

  If you have the financial wherewithal to do so, sign up for some paid subscriptions. Have a magazine or two that is a favorite of yours arrive by mail, have a fruit-of-the-month club subscription arrive, have a subscription that gets you out of the house to attend a concert or play series. It is good to have some pleasant surprises to come home to, or the excuse to get you out of the house to attend a play or concert. We often will go, if we paid for it, so a paid subscription does help get us out of the house, which is our mantra, to be *doing*, to keep moving.

MILEPOST TIP: Managing Expectations

EXPECT STOP AND GO. Expectations for the road to your new future, should be realistic. Although each grieving person has a unique road map, like a fingerprint or snowflake in which no two are alike, anticipate moments of stop and go. Expect times you will have no trouble "moving on" or "letting go" followed closely by times of "holding on" or "not letting go." Managing expectations means you will need to be prepared to encounter the red, yellow, and green traffic lights on the road to your new self. Remember, we progress at our own speed.

Letting In: Dating?

One obvious aspect of moving forward is making the decision to start dating again after the loss of a significant other or spouse. It is common for grievers to be asked, "Are you thinking of dating again?" Be mindful that after your loss you may not be fully yourself, and you may need more time before answering this question. So, tread gently if you consider this possibility moving forward.

- **Companionship v. Dating**

  For many, companionship is the greatest loss. Companionship rather than dating is the objective for many grievers. It can be difficult to navigate the fine line between the two, as one party may want more out of a relationship. The best policy is to be open about your intentions. Two people, especially those who have suffered loss, can be open and honest and let the other know that companionship is his or her interest. This can be a relief to both parties.

- **Pros and Cons of Dating**
  - **PROS:** For some it is a no-brainer, with comments like "I am no good at doing life on my own" or "I need a person in my life to love." If this is you, then moving forward with your life you may have the goal of dating again clearly in mind.
  - **CONS:** For some it is simply having no interest in dating. For others it may be considered a sign of disrespect to the deceased. Others have been concerned about the signal that dating sends to the rest of the world; perhaps they will be judged. One man reasoned, "If I start dating, people will think my marriage was not the all-time best which I've already said it was."

- **Doing the Dating Game**
  - **"You Need to Get Out There Again" v. "It's Too Soon"**
    When is it the right time to start dating again? The correct answer is there is no exact "right" time. It will always be too early or too late depending on someone weighing in on your life. You are in charge of your life and you have to do what is best for you, but expect well-meaning friends and family members to put in their two-cents.
  - **Get the Word Out**
    Let friends and family know you are interested in dating again, but be aware your decision may provoke mixed reviews. Attend more social and community events where you will have an opportunity to meet people. Consider creating an online dating profile if you are interested in reentering the world of dating. As there are people with not-the-right intentions online, approach with caution including background checks on people you do not know.
  - **Dating, Know Yourself, Know Your Hurdles**
    First there are the psychological hurdles. For many it may be the first time since middle school or high school that they went on a date with someone other than their loved one. This brings up the psychological hurdles of "Am I worthy?" or "Am I disloyal?". After that come the feelings of inadequacy. I am no longer twenty-one, am I even "marketable" or "desirable" to anyone anymore? Then come the emotional hurdles. One man admitted that the woman he is dating said to him, "I don't think you are over grieving your wife." Take it in your own time, take it slow, and be willing to hit the pause button and take a break. Anyone with an ounce of empathy will understand your reentry into dating may take a little time to smooth out the wrinkles. If you're ready for companionship, take it one step at a time.

Truths from the Road: Dating and the Pendulum of Grief

Dating

"I'm not sure I can risk having my heart broken again, by falling in love with another person."

"I have joy. I'm moving forward. I'm not stuck. I will keep my first wife in my heart for the rest of my life."

"My girlfriend thinks I'm still grieving my wife."

Where are you on the pendulum of grief?

"My brother says I need to get over it."

"When my wife was dying, she told me I wouldn't be able to survive on my own and that she has picked out her replacement for me."

"I keep getting asked, 'It's been over three months now, don't you think it is time to move on?'"

"Isn't it time to get out there and start dating?"

The pendulum swings, and you may hear the following:

"Isn't it a little soon to start dating, wouldn't that be disrespectful?"

Referencing dating, a daughter stated, "Way too soon, Dad."

"I don't want to meet the woman you are dating," said another daughter.

"It's not even been a year, that's too soon."

- **LETTING IN: Open to Marriage?**

  Considering marriage again after the loss of a partner can seem as foreign as looking up the words "Will you marry me?" in a foreign language phrase book. The concept of marrying again, even the thought of it, can be a gift from your deceased spouse. If you are a widower and considering remarriage after the death of your spouse, then you know that it is the legacy of your spouse that makes you want to consider marriage again. A priest had to say this about a couple who married after loss: "Jim loved marriage so much that he just couldn't live without it. This was a tribute to his first wife Diana who had died. This is the gift that Diana gave to Jim, to want to live the rest of his years on Earth married again."

SCENIC OVERVIEW: Your View from the Car Window

Roll down your window and let the fresh air blow. If you have a convertible or a motorcycle, extra gold stars for you. What is the view from your window, what does the landscape look like? You have started your journey and the mile markers are flying by. Perhaps this is you: You are in the zone. You are fully present. There was a long stretch of miles where your mind was completely free, and there was not a pit in your stomach or throat from your loss. Pure unbridled joy of being on the road. You are on this journey, you expect good things, you know you are going to make new discoveries—new discoveries about the land we live in and new discoveries about yourself. Prepare to be surprised. Fasten your seat belts. Hooray, you are on our way!

DOING: Making the Calendar Your Friend

Time has no divisions to mark its passage, there is never a thunderstorm or blare of trumpets to announce the beginning of a new month or year.
—Thomas Mann

They always say time changes things, but you actually have to change them yourself.
—Andy Warhol

The "Gotcha" Calendar: Your Year of Firsts and Beyond

What are your "GOTCHA DATES"? Gotcha dates are those days on the calendar that will be especially challenging to you after your loss. These are public holidays and birthdays and anniversaries that have always brought you joy. After loss you should also note on your calendar the more problematic days, such as the anniversary of your loved one's death or the anniversary day of the diagnosis. These days are like the speed bumps and potholes on your destination road, and the following are suggestions to help prepare you for these potentially stressful days.

- **"GOTCHA DATES" AND HOLIDAYS**

  First identify your gotcha dates and holidays on this calendar including birthdays, anniversaries, and every holiday that has meaning to you and the one you lost.

- **IMPORTANT DATE STRATEGIES**

  Begin work on a strategy in advance of each special landmark date. Plan how you will spend the day on the anniversary of your loved one's death or birthday.

  o Spend an intentional thirty minutes in the morning alone, giving thanks and sharing gratitude to and for your loved one.

- Perhaps honor your loved one's legacy by planting flowers or a tree, or providing some service to others to honor your loved one.

- Many people say they like solitude on these days, others want to make sure they have others around. Some want a balance of both.

- You decide, but have your plan in advance so you are not worrying about stepping on this upcoming "landmine." The lead up to these gotcha dates is usually worse than the actual day. It may seem counterintuitive, but if proactive steps are taken, these days can be very heartwarming and healing.

Creating Your Road Map Calendar Placeholders

- No blank calendar allowed. Your goal should be to have specific events to look forward to in the future, something meaningful and pleasurable to you that is on your calendar. The dread of looking at a blank calendar can also motivate you to work weekly on the exercises in this book to build your road map calendar.

- After marking the gotcha dates on your calendar, write the dates of events in which you know you have commitments. You may already know about a family reunion, a wedding, or a graduation ceremony that you may be expected to or want to attend. Put these on your calendar. Your calendar will probably have a mix of routine appointments to the doctor or dentist, filled with any regularly scheduled hair appointments or "necessary" self-care luxuries, such as appointments for a manicure or massage.

- **WRITE IN PENCIL:** Your life after loss often feels like it is written in pencil. If needed, write on your calendar in pencil. You have the right to change your mind.

- **MAKING IT STICK:** Use sticky notes. Write your planned activity that does not yet have a hard date, and place it on the calendar. This is your calendar placeholder. If you need to change the date, move it forward or back, simply move the sticky note.

DOING: Holidays, and the Calendar

Holiday grief is real. Holidays can create grief on steroids. The holidays are on your calendar so make plans on how you want to approach them. Included is a Permission Slip in the exercise section of this book to use if needed. The important takeaway for holidays is to acknowledge the loss of the person, and to *keep their spirit alive in your heart.* Use the person's name and announce to the family at your holiday gathering that you would like to lift up the legacy of this person for a moment. Then move on to your celebrations. It is absolutely okay if there are a few tears, but encourage laughter at the same time by recounting a special story or two. This is all part of healthy healing.

Truths from the Road: The Holidays

"The holidays are hard, double hard, as my mother's birthday is Christmas."

A son said: "Mother's Day was really hard, I cried for two hours."

ROAD SCHOLAR ASSIGNMENT: Permission Slip for the Holidays

Complete a Permission Slip to allow yourself to make changes to your holiday celebrations this year. You are giving yourself permission to modify or even skip the holidays this year. This may be the time to start new traditions. Write down what you are thinking, sign and date it. Put it on your refrigerator or share with family and friends. This will empower you to do things differently for the holidays this year, if that is your wish. PERMISSION GRANTED.

DOING: "Get Outta Town" Thinking Travel?

Literally, make plans to "get outta town" and travel. Plan a trip, no matter how short or long. Travel changes us. Particularly if you take in different locales and cultures. A trip can be a healing balm after loss. You may return home with a fresh view to make changes in your home, changes in your day-to-day living. Or, you might simply be glad to be back in your safe haven, your harbor. But remember, ships are built for the open seas, not for the safety of the harbor. By land, sea, or air (or all three)—what will be your travel plan?

Truths from the Road: Travel

"I went to Antarctica with a travel group as a single person."

"My husband and I loved to travel, so I am taking his ashes to all the places we would travel to- I'm calling it my 'William Tour'."

Take a Road Trip, Road Trip Ideas

Yes, I know this book uses a road trip as a metaphor for your journey to healing and renewal after loss. So, brilliantly thinking, "Eureka!"—the light bulb goes on! Why not go on a self-actualizing road trip that mirrors the figurative road trip that you are on! As the old song says, "nothing could be finer than to be in Carolina in the morning," so where do you want to wake up next to shake things up? Think small, medium, or large, even grandiose in scale. Maybe you will get a true old-fashioned map and highlight or draw on it. Highlight the roads you plan to take and the roadside attractions you would like to visit. This is your road map and you can do what you want!

- **The One Day "Change of Scenery" Road Trip**
  Say to yourself, "An outing will do me good." Then set your sights "to make a day of it" as soon as possible. If no one is available to join you, go on your own. Solitary trips are healthy for healing and can also serve as a remembrance opportunity. Visit a location that takes you out of your normal everyday experience.

- **Try an Overnight or Weekend Road Trip**
  Consider a weekend getaway. Bring an open mind, open heart, and perhaps an audio book and road trip music. Less adventurous? Try a themed or scenic bus tour, there are many from which to choose.

- **Friends and Family Road Trip Tour**
  Plan a road trip that may last several days or weeks to visit friends and relatives, revisit important places in your past, or attend class reunions.

- **The Bucket List Trip**
  What is on your bucket list? A famous music festival? A major sports event? A site of natural scenic beauty, such as Niagara Falls, the Grand Canyon, or New England in autumn? Make plans to visit when you are ready and able.

- **Not Sure Where to Go? Perhaps Memory Lane**

  You may want to consider a trip down memory lane, revisiting a place or two from your childhood or teenage years. Visit nostalgic places that may be therapeutic for you, from playgrounds and schools to places where you lived and played.

- **The No-destination Serendipity Road Trip**

  Open mind travel. Head out without a plan or notion where you want to end up. Soak up whatever you see and find. Your travel motto will be spontaneity and you are free to simply enjoy the ride. Expect the unexpected and bring a double dose of patience. Your no-destination excursion may be just the ticket for your road ahead to healing.

- **Reentry, Coming Home after a Road Trip**

  Grievers report that it takes a little time to adjust to being home after being away. It can be another reminder of the true reality of your loss, arriving home to an empty home without your loved one. Asked if they would go again, the response was a resounding "Yes!"

ROAD SCHOLAR ASSIGNMENT: My One Big Thing Visualization

Dream big, let your mind take you to your One Big Thing. Place a picture or a photo out of a magazine of one big thing you would like in your future. Place it in your notebook, a place, person, or thing to work toward, your personal goal. One woman who lost her husband is beginning to dream of starting over in Hawaii. She would have to sell her house and possessions and rent a place in Hawaii but would be happy to live simply and work at a routine job that pays the bills. She knows that it will take time to realize this dream, but she is motivated to clean her house and purge her possessions in readiness to put her house on the market. This can be a one-year, three-year, or "for the rest of my life" interest or passion. Your One Big Thing can be relatively small, but for you it is big at this juncture. Something to build on. If you know your One Big Thing, that can be your default answer to all who ask, "What are you going to do now?"

Journal Thoughts _____

_____

_____

Truths from the Road: Doing Life after Loss

The Smallest Things

"I began cooking for myself, and healthily, not just eating junk food and fast food at a drive thru."

"I bought a puppy and that was the best thing I ever did."

"I'm on an amaryllis watch, as I expect it to be blooming on the anniversary of my wife's death."

"I adopted a cat from a friend who died, and I get a lot of joy from my cat."

Everyday Coping

"There are everyday things I am scared to death to do."

"Listening to music after my mother died brings out the best and the worst, music is more beautiful and more sad, all at the same time."

"My husband is not in bed but I curl up with his pillow"

Conclusion

If you have reached this far and have not started any of the exercises in this book, this would be a good time to begin. Start an exercise that you can do NOW, not later. YOUR CHOICE: Choose a TAKE FIVE five-minute or thirty-minute exercise or assignment. *Vroom, vroom!* Finally, the following quote from Mother Teresa was on the wall of one of our hospice patients, a young man with a wonderful spirit:

Do It Anyway

People are often unreasonable, irrational, and self-centered. Forgive them anyway.

If you are kind, people may accuse you of selfish, ulterior motives. Be kind anyway.

If you are successful, you will win some unfaithful friends and some genuine enemies. Succeed anyway.

If you are honest and sincere people may deceive you. Be honest and sincere anyway.

What you spend years creating, others could destroy overnight. Create anyway.

Give the best you have, and it will never be enough. Give your best anyway.

In the final analysis, it is between you and God. It was never between you and them anyway.

—Mother Teresa

ROAD SCHOLAR ASSIGNMENT: The DOING Thirty-Day Challenge

On your calendar simply check Yes or No for the next thirty days to the following questions. Did I get out of the house today? Yes/No. Did I try something new today? Yes/No. Did I get out of my comfort zone today and reach out to another person? Yes/No. Practice this for thirty days and this will become a habit which will help you on your road to renewal. Be aware that we are preprogrammed to revert to our default setting, that is to stay in our comfort zone.

Journal Thoughts _____

_____

_____

_____

_____

_____

_____

_____

_____

_____

_____

Part 3
BEING—The Inner Road

What lies behind us and what lies before us are tiny matters, compared to what lies within us.

—Henry S. Haskins

If there is to be any peace it will come through being, not having.

—Henry Miller

If you don't like something, change it; if you can't change it, change the way you think about it.

—Mary Engelbreit

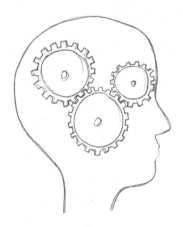

Did you know that all of us on this planet share the same last name? Yes, we are all a "Being," the most common surname in the world! Since we as humans share this in common, let us take some time to see how we can make the most of our "being" here on planet Earth.

On your road trip through and beyond grief, perhaps the toughest part of the journey is focusing on yourself, YOU—the one who is sitting behind the wheel. As you travel forward, you will be resurfacing your Inner Road of Being in preparation for you to reach your destination of healing and renewal. This section on BEING focuses on the mind and emotional underpinnings of the road through and beyond grief. It is often stated that the mind is the final frontier, and understanding and managing your mind and emotions will be your most significant challenge.

This section of your road trip is meant to be one of self-discovery, with the focus on looking inward and engaging with yourself. This is your road less traveled, BEING: The Inner Road. The focus on being is best labelled as the non-doing section of your road trip, but with the understanding that to be intentional about *being* will require some internal *doing* on your part. In the pages that follow, we are deliberately moving from your To-Do list to your To-Be list—from Being to Becoming. Perhaps this section on BEING may be more difficult than DOING, so that is why DOING came first to help build some momentum before getting to the hard work of searching within. To know where you are going, you will need to know where you came from, which means to accept and acknowledge your loss. You need to be both intentional, and at times, to be still, to see where you are headed. Ideally, you will fluctuate from "doing" to "being" and back, continually.

REMEMBER: I invite you to slow down, brake, and take the appropriate exit when it presents itself. You may want to address one or more of the attributes of Being. Enjoy the ride and the view, you may be surprised by some of the scenic overlooks on this journey. Keep on driving through if this following section is not helpful or important to you.

BEING OR DOING? Why Not Both!

The great business of life is to be, to do, to do without, and to depart.
—John Morley

It's not enough to be industrious. So are the ants. What are you industrious about?
—Henry David Thoreau

Some grief experts advise that after loss the focus should be on the inner emotional and spiritual spring of well-being that is deep down in all of us. I call this "Being." Fortunately, the road ahead has two lanes, so be prepared to travel both and to change lanes from Being to Doing on this journey.

Know Thyself

I think, therefore I am.
—René Descartes

What is the hardest task in the world? To think.
—Ralph Waldo Emerson

We know what we are now, but know not what we may become.
—William Shakespeare, *Hamlet*

It is well known that the ancient Greeks traveled to the Oracle at Delphi to seek wisdom and knowledge. Above the entrance, the phrase "Know Thyself" was inscribed, which philosophers have interpreted as the need to know firsthand who we are as individuals before we can understand the world in which we live. Socrates expanded on that phrase to teach: "The unexamined life is not worth living." For us to move forward on our road trip we must honestly look inward to understand who we are first, to help map our Road to Renewal.

What does "Know Thyself" mean? It means to understand yourself, to know your likes and dislikes, your preferences, desires, and goals, and ultimately what makes you tick, your purpose in life. It also is knowing your triggers, what creates stress and anxiety for you, and what drains you and what uplifts you.

ROAD SCHOLAR ASSIGNMENT: Know Thyself

Your significant loss is also an important opportunity to learn about yourself. Take a few minutes to reflect what insights you have learned about yourself since your loss. In your notebook, write your response to the following: *What have you learned about yourself as a result of your loss? What has surprised you the most?*

Who Am I? Your Inner-self Archaeological Dig

You road I enter upon and look around, I believe you are not all that is here, I believe that much unseen is also here.

—Walt Whitman, "Song of the Open Road"

Your goal will be to move to your inner sacred and higher ground by gaining a better understanding of yourself and the world in which you live.

Who am I?

Am I worthy?

_____

Do I feel worthy of being allowed to have happiness and joy again?

_____

Do I feel I will ever be good enough, or deserve to be happy again?

_____

Do I feel regretful or remorseful for events leading up to and after my loss?

_____

Do I feel guilty or shameful for events leading up to and after my loss?

_____

The Blank Page

This page is left intentionally blank.

THIS EMPTY SPACE is brought to you by your INNER BEING.

"Being" Building: Are You Under Construction?

A bird does not sing because it has an answer, it sings because it has a song.

— Joan Walsh Anglund, *A Cup of Sun*

Being is the great explainer.

—Henry David Thoreau

To be alive—is Power—
Existence—in itself—
Without a further function—
Omnipotence—Enough

—Emily Dickinson

Do You Have a "To-Be" List?

As you read the pages in this section, start to think about what you may want to include in your "To-Be" list. Dare to get in touch with your inner self, your emotional self. People need to feel emotions, as "feeling is healing." The inner emotional workout is just as important as the physical "no pain, no gain" workout mantra.

ROAD SCHOLAR ASSIGNMENT: Writing Your "To-Be" List

As you are renewing yourself after loss, take a few minutes to write in your notebook what you would like to include on your "To-Be" list. Select several of the topics in this section that resonate with you, or those of your own choice, and explain why these are important. Highlighting these specific areas here for additional emphasis or work brings these top of mind for you to spend quality time on them. Your "To-Be" list may include areas that you want to increase, such as cultivating gratitude and hopefulness, and areas that you want to decrease, such as guilt and regret. Viewing your responses in writing can be very powerful and helpful.

INCREASE	DECREASE
Topic	Topic
Why?	Why?
Topic	Topic
Why?	Why?

Life after Loss

Your life after loss often may feel like it is written in pencil, easily rubbed out. Welcome to temporary permanence. Your personal life, your "being" is life in transition. Be patient. *How do you feel alive again?* Start with the basics. The most basic of basics is nature. Slow down, still yourself, and breathe. We have already won the lottery of birth and are alive. So, how do we harness this great news that we have won the human lottery and are fully alive? How do we become fully energized and engaged, and approach life with enthusiasm again? How do we add a little energy? How do we add a little pizzazz?

Know That "You Are Your Weather"

When you come out of the storm, you won't be the same person who walked in. That's what this storm is all about.

—Haruki Murakami

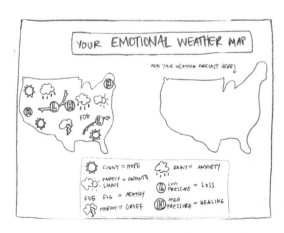

Be aware of the "internal" weather patterns inside you. "You are your own weather" was a motto and life lesson that one of our patients passed on to her children and to me. That you *own* your emotions, your inner weather. No matter what the physical weather brings, whether there is rain, sleet, or snow, you can have sunshine inside. It can be helpful to know that you are not powerless, and that you do have some control over your internal weather. Grief resembles the weather in so many ways, it is constantly changing, often suddenly and unexpectedly. The following characteristics and attributes can greatly affect your internal weather, and hopefully, you will understand and embrace your personal weather to help you on your road to renewal.

BEING: Building after Loss

Unlike the snail we carry our homes within us which enables us to fly or to stay, to enjoy each.

—John Cage

Laughter and tears are meant to turn the wheels of the same machinery of sensibility; one is wind-power, and the other water-power, that is all.

—Oliver Wendell Holmes, Sr., *The Autocrat of the Breakfast-Table*

The following characteristics of BEING are designed to be appetizers, to whet your appetite for those areas that are of most interest to you. The first section highlights the positive emotions of BEING that hopefully you will be able to IN-CREASE in your life. This is followed by a section on the negative emotions of BEING that ideally you can be aware of and try to DECREASE their hold on your life. Books are written on each topic and I recommend further reading and reflection for those areas that are of interest.

INCREASE: Arrive Empty, Fill Yourself Up

THE ABCs OF BEING: Attributes in Alphabetical Order

Affirmation: Your Daily Affirmation

We need to become as positive as possible to develop the strength to confront face-to-face the challenges of loss. You may want to adopt a daily affirmation statement, such as the sample below, to help firm up your positivity. Please modify to fit your interests and needs. Write it in your notebook or place it somewhere you can see every morning.

DAILY AFFIRMATION STATEMENT

I am thankful for life.

I am hopeful that today will be a good day.

I am forgiving myself and others.

I am trusting that I am on the road to finding joy again.

Aging: What's in Your Basket?

Anyone who stops learning is old, whether at twenty or eighty. Anyone who keeps learning stays young. The greatest thing in life is to keep your mind young.

—Henry Ford

Time deals gently only with those who take it gently.

—Anatole France

Age is a mindset, not a number. Aging is an adjustment, not a barrier. Your road to healing and renewal is age neutral. The road is open to all no matter your age or circumstances. *What's in your lifespan basket?* Do you expect to live another ten years, another twenty years or more? Whatever is in your lifespan basket, now is the time to maximize the time you have left. With aging we can grieve the passing of our peak optimal performance, appearance, or mobility. It is normal for a time to grieve the life we had wished or hoped to have lived, thus feeling sadness and regret for missed or failed opportunities. These laments are normal. What is important is accepting what happened in the past. Acceptance is key for us to be content in the present and to make a positive future.

Like fine wine, maybe there are some advantages to aging. There are studies which show that those over the age of seventy can live very productive and happy lives, often without much of the stress of those half their age. With the aging process usually comes an accumulation of losses, but despite diminishing abilities and physical limitations, aging seems to provide valuable skills to help us cope better after loss. Wisdom and life experiences make aging a beneficial characteristic in coping with change and loss. Working with hospice patients and their families, I am constantly struck by how much those considered well advanced in age have to impart, inspire, and teach us all.

Aesthetics: Sustenance for the Soul

Beauty is whatever gives joy.

—Edna St. Vincent Millay

There are always flowers for those who want to see them.

—Henri Matisse

Aesthetics simply means appreciating and enjoying beauty. Surrounding yourself with simple beauty can lift your spirits and countenance and be a counterweight to grief and loss. We do not always have control over the big things, but we can make sure the gift of beauty is around us. Sometimes it is as simple as taking stock of your surroundings, stepping outside to appreciate the beauty of the sky or the shadows on a building. Inside your mind and physical surroundings, create a place that can be your sanctuary, your haven with beauty surrounding you. Remember, beauty is in the eye of the beholder and can be the simplest of items, a plant or vase of flowers. The appreciation of small, meaningful, and beautiful possessions can make a huge difference. Aesthetics is our way of refreshing our senses; keeping beauty at hand does not have to cost anything.

MILEPOST TIP: Keep an Important Memento Visible

Consider placing an important memento of beauty or meaning nearby in a prominent location that you see and come in contact with daily. It could be an ink pen, an umbrella, a teacup, a stone, or embroidered napkin. This special something, a souvenir (French for *memory*), will inspire you and give you comfort.

Aspiration: To What Do You Aspire?

Aspire comes from the Latin phrase "to breathe upon" and is meant to channel one's desire to achieve something of importance in the future. Whether we are breathed upon by God or a higher power, we all have the ability to aspire, that is we have the hope that we too can experience joy and happiness again. This book is aspirational, knowing that recovering from loss is a process over time. Today you may not be ready for some of the suggested concepts and exercises, but it is important for you to know that your Aspire Superhighway exists and is available when you are ready.

Balance: Finding Your Balance Again

Life is like a bicycle. To keep your balance, you must keep moving.
—Albert Einstein

Are you feeling out of alignment? No doubt you may have lost your balance and feel out of alignment after your loss. Our journey together is to get back on solid ground again, to create a firm foundation to rebuild your life. One woman stated after her loss, "I feel like I am out of balance. I become frustrated easier than I ever have been in my life." Some have asked, "Am I grieving too slow?" Another wondered, "Am I actually doing too well? I am waiting for the second shoe to drop." Are you wearing a scarlet letter, a red "G" for "Griever" feeling that you have been banished from the world around you? Are you *Goldilocks grieving*, feeling that you are grieving too much or not enough, or too slow or too fast, in search for that perfect "just right" amount? You will get your balance back as you bounce back.

100

Change/Time: Life Is Embracing Change

Time heals griefs and quarrels, for we change and are no longer the same persons.

—Blaise Pascal

For the times they are a-changin'

—Bob Dylan

All is flux; nothing stays still.

—Heraclitus

Life after loss is change. The good news is that this pain, this deflating situation you find yourself in, is not permanent. Nothing in life is permanent, and that is what makes daily life so vital and inspiring.

Life Is Change

Life is a series of adjustments to reach balance.

Life is reorganizing and reevaluating.

Life is a shock absorber.

Life is recalculating, your internal GPS.

Life is evolving, your heart is evolving.

Contentment: Getting to "Enough"

For I have learned, in whatsoever state I am, therewith to be content.

—Philippians 4:11, KJV

Contentment is in your control, not easily attained but available to you. If you can experience joy, available readily to all at no cost, and if you can cultivate gratitude, you can experience a full life ahead, a life of contentment. Living a life, where one never has enough, is like a thirst that is insatiable. If we are not careful and have a mindset that we do not have enough, or that we never will because of our loss, sets us up for a difficult future, and is clearly a life-limiting prognosis.

Continuity: Continuing Relationship

Change and *continuity* are the two main threads that run throughout human history and the same is true for you. Death has brought great change, but you will look to continue as many aspects of your life as possible. One area of continuity that you should consider retaining is a continuing spiritual relationship with your loved one. Many of the bereaved I work with speak to their deceased loved one every day or write letters to them to describe what is going on in their lives daily. This is natural and normal, and is a part of healthy healing from your loss. Your relationship continues, but it is a different, evolving, and new relationship as it moves from the physical to the spiritual. Some of you will have dreams and visions of your loved one and some of you won't have them, that is fine too. Your continuing relationship with your loved one will change over time, but don't hesitate to do what feels right to you. *Love endures and continues after death.* One woman stated that despite her grief, gratitude permeated her being, and despite the loss, "I somehow feel I'm still taking part in the life we created together."

Creativity: Finding Your Inner Child

Travel "back to the future" and relearn how to be childlike. First, you may need to unlearn a lot of what the world has been teaching you. After loss may be the perfect time for you to reunite with your inner child. Creativity can be such a great outlet for anyone, particularly adults on a journey beyond grief. Be brave enough to express yourself in writing, or through art or music. Perfectionism  or even being good at it is not the point. Get some colored pencils, chalk, markers, paints, and paper and express what is in your heart. You could even finger paint with dirt mixed with a little water. You will feel better. Any outlet of creativity is therapeutic on your road to renewal.

EPIPHANY ALERT:
Expect Aha Moments

Be expectant of an aha moment. Once grief happens, you have hit the RESET button, and the opportunity for an epiphany or aha moment will appear to you. One woman reported, "My epiphany moment came to me two weeks ago when I told myself I am no longer going to say 'I should have' or 'it should have been.' I am in acceptance of the past and at peace." Be open to an aha moment being revealed to you.

Faith: Your Powerful Insurance Policy

Seeds of faith are always within us; sometimes it takes a crisis to nourish and encourage their growth.
—Susan L. Taylor

Fifty miles to go and she was running low on faith and gasoline
—B. James, G. Sampson, and H. Lindsey, "Jesus, Take the Wheel"

Faith can be your *insurance policy* of protection—your assurance that you will be OK. For best results, have *faith* as your travel companion—faith that you will have the strength and ability to renew and reinvent yourself on the road ahead, faith that you will get through this, and that *this too shall pass.* If you have a religious faith or come from a nonpracticing faith tradition, you may find a renewed interest in your faith after loss. Faith is a powerful asset to have on this journey. One woman told me her key to getting through and beyond grief was the "Three *F*s: **F**aith, **F**riends, and **F**amily."

Forgiveness Is "For Giving"

Forgive us our debts, as we forgive our debtors.

—Matthew 6:12, KJV

To err is human; to forgive, divine.

—Alexander Pope

To understand is to forgive, even oneself.

—Alexander Chase

Give the gift of forgiving to yourself and to others. Airlines encourage adults in emergencies to take the oxygen mask to save their lives first, before helping others. The same is true about forgiveness. Forgive yourself first.

The paradox is that as you forgive yourself or even someone who is not "deserving" of forgiveness, the additional burdens of anger, guilt, and sorrow that you are carrying seem to lift almost immediately.

Forgive yourself, your loved one, and anyone else in your life. Lighten your load. One less bag to carry.

Gratitude: Priming the Gratitude Pump

Gratitude doesn't change the scenery. It merely washes clean the glass you look through so you can clearly see the colors.

—Richelle E. Goodrich

A single thankful thought towards heaven is the most perfect of all prayers.

—Gotthold Ephraim Lessing

We express gratitude when we are grateful or thankful. Consider gratitude as a super additive fuel to put in your "Being" gas tank. Those who have suffered loss tell me they get an immediate feeling of well-being once they are able to express gratitude for the life of their loved one and gratitude for life itself. This is the *gratitude bump* that you get at the Gratitude Pump. Come to the Gratitude Filling Station. Come in empty and fill yourself up. Fill yourself up with gratitude. For the rest of your life, prime the Gratitude Pump and experience the magic of how expressing your gratitude can lift your overall spirit and emotional well-being.

ROAD SCHOLAR ASSIGNMENT: The Take-Five Gratitude Challenge

Take Five each day. Five minutes, or even five seconds, to give thanks for your gift of life. Take Five daily to give thanks for the time and love you shared with your loved one, even though this time may seem too short. Start today, by adding the Gratitude Five into your daily life and you will soon be strengthening your gratitude muscles which will result in a greatly improved positive outlook on life. Add the Take-Five Gratitude Challenge to your calendar today.

Heaven and the Afterlife: The Ultimate Destination

Believe in something for another World, but don't be too set on what it is, and then you won't start out that life with a disappointment.

—Will Rogers

Many of those I speak to after loss are comforted by the concept of heaven or an afterlife. There is comfort in the belief that death is not the end, but rather the beginning of eternal life and that we will be reunited with our loved

---

Journal Thoughts _____

_____

_____

_____

_____

_____

_____

_____

_____

ones after death. Heaven or a version of the afterlife is viewed by most I speak with as their ultimate destination. The concept of heaven can be comforting even to children. One girl who is eight years old did not seem to be too frightened by her grandmother's death: "Granny is going to Heaven House." Not to have this belief can make the grieving journey a little more arduous. Near the end of his life, Steve Jobs, the founder of Apple, told his biographer, Walter Isaacson, that he is hopeful something survives us after death, but ruminated on the possibility of an on-off switch. He said, "Maybe that's why I never liked to put on-off switches on Apple devices."

Higher Power and Spirituality: Are You Powered by a Higher Power?

There is a God-shaped vacuum in the heart of each man which cannot be satisfied by any created thing but only by God the Creator, made known through Jesus Christ.

—Blaise Pascal

Be still, and know that I am God.

—Psalm 46:10, KJV

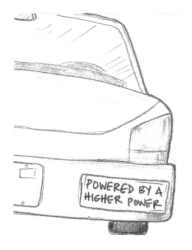

If you believe there is something greater than us in this universe then you believe in a higher power. Whether God is your higher power or something not of religious origins, being powered by a higher power can be very helpful to you on this journey beyond grief. Do you view your grief journey as a pilgrimage? A pilgrimage to healing, even a spiritual pilgrimage? As a writer, I felt "summoned" by God, my higher power, to write this book. To tell the story inspired by those I work with daily so it can be of help to others, just as I have been so greatly helped and blessed by others. The secret of our healing is to use our loss for good.

What's God or a higher power got to do with it? For those who are believers, life after loss is too difficult a journey to face on your own, and requires an assist from above. Many of you who have faith in God or a higher power are comforted by the promise "surely I am with you always" (Matthew 28:20, NIV). After the loss of her husband, one woman said, "OK, God, what's our next adventure? Let's go!" Another man stated, "God has helped me through my grief; I wouldn't have made it otherwise." Your road trip will be energized if your internal motor is turbocharged by a HIGHER POWER.

Hope: Hope Revisited

Where there is no hope there can be no endeavor.

—Samuel Johnson

The HOPE Acrostic: Reprise of Grief's Big Four

H—Heart: Your loved one is in your *heart* forever.

O—Only: *Only* those who have truly loved are the lucky ones.

P—Permission: Give yourself *permission* to live life to the fullest, this you owe your loved one.

E—Expectation: *Expect* to feel joy again, *expect* that some of your best days are still ahead.

Inspiration: Strive to Be Inspired

To move forward, we need inspiration. How do we get inspiration? Sit and it will come. Look and it will come. Write and it will come. Walk and it will come. It may not be inspiration with all capital letters and in neon lights, but it may be just enough inspiration to help you make a decision, no matter how small, that helps you on your road ahead.

Joy: Joy Happens

The fact is always obvious much too late, but the most singular difference between happiness and joy is that happiness is a solid and joy is a liquid.

—J. D. Salinger

Happiness makes up in height for what it lacks in length.

—Robert Frost

Perhaps the secret to life is to be content and at peace. But what about joy? To be fully human we need joy in our lives. Even after loss, be on the lookout for "joy bursts" or isolated outbreaks of joy. Recognize that you have been visited by a joy burst, a spark of joy, and be thankful for this fleeting arrival of joy. As humans we are hardwired to experience joy, it is internal and not dependent on our individual situation or circumstances. Know that joy is available to you today and over time these joy bursts will visit you more often and stay longer. Expect to be in wonderment that you too will be visited by one or more sparks of joy which float through the sky.

Which comes first: joy or gratitude? (Grief's version of chicken and egg.) Practice gratitude and joy will follow. Be open to joy and gratitude will show up. If you are one of those who have said: "I don't think I will ever get my joy back"—be patient, joy is on its way.

Is There a Formula for Happiness and Joy?

Why not try a little FGH?

FGH: Forgiveness for the past, Gratitude for the present, Hope for the future.

Laughter: Now Is the Time to Get Your Laughter Back

The most wasted of all days is one without laughter.

—e. e. cummings

If I am not allowed to laugh in heaven, I don't want to go there.

—Martin Luther

Laughter is the brush that sweeps away the cobwebs of your heart.

—Mort Walker

No one seems to feel like laughing after loss. For some it can seem disrespectful to the memory of a loved one to have laughter. When is the time to "get my laughter back?" The answer is *now*. Laughter is the balm for many ills and is good for one's health, even more so after loss. Laughter is a body relaxer and stress reliever. Laughter and humor can be our psychological armor. Hopefully you will seek out laughter on your road ahead.

What makes you laugh? Whatever it is, increase the dose. Up the laugh track. When our daughter was going through her cancer journey, I was shocked when her doctor walked into her hospital room and told us to turn the TV channel to a comedy channel, essentially prescribing us much needed laughter. With serious stuff still ahead of you, I, too, echo this advice, LAUGH and LAUGH OFTEN. In any group I lead with grievers, I share my three "L" rules: Love, Lifting up the legacy of the loved one, and Laughter. We try to laugh enough to sustain ourselves through the week until our next time together.

Love: The Greatest of All

And now these three remain: faith, hope and love. But the greatest of these is love.

—1 Corinthians 13:13, NIV

There is no remedy for love but to love more.

—Henry David Thoreau

Consider letting love into your life again. If you are one of the fortunate ones who have loved and have been loved, how do you embrace love again after loss? Love is defined by Merriam-Webster as "an intense feeling of deep affection." To love is to be vulnerable, to risk having your heart broken. Often the meaning of this word has been hijacked to signify romantic love. There are many types of love, including love of family, love of friends, love of country, and love of a pet or animal. How will you let love into your life if romantic love is unwanted or seems out of reach? One woman was known for telling her family: "All I want for Christmas is love, love, love, love, love." Love all, love life, love your past, love your present, and love your future.

Memories: Thanks for the Memories

Thanks for the memory.
—theme song of Bob Hope

Our memory is a more perfect world than the universe: it gives back life to those who no longer exist.
—Guy de Maupassant

We are our memories. Memories give us our framework to face the world. Try to cultivate your happy place of memories that you can go to easily and often. Even death cannot separate us from our memories. We have our memories and it is important to cherish them. After the shock of loss, or a long end-of-life decline, we may need to reach back to cultivate those positive and happy memories from the past. The good news is that over time, positive memories are more likely to stick with us long term than any unpleasant or bad memories.

Remembering his life and wife, one man expressed, "I know how to be lucky. My wife and I were together fifty-seven years, we worked together for twenty-five years, I pursued her for fifteen years, finally caught her and we were married for forty-two. I sure was lucky for a long time." One of our recent patients, a successful man who had lost his wife several years ago, was well known for telling everyone he met, "Marrying my wife was the best decision I ever made." I encourage you to capture one, two, or three special memories that summarize your special relationship, and keep them alive in your heart. Be sure to share these memories with others too.

Mindfulness: Minding the Moment

Living in the moment is harder than it sounds. When grieving it is easy to be swallowed whole by the past and overwhelmed about the future. How do we *mind the moment*? How can we *live in the moment*? Being fully awake to life by focusing on the present moment is the aim of mindfulness. Our emphasis on BEING means we need to make strides to learn to be fully pres-

108

ent. We should learn to develop awareness of the present moment, not every moment of the day, but at least once a day when you can quiet your inner self and be intentional about shedding external noise and disquiet. Simply to be present in the here and now, the *present*. The contemplative life. From silence to solitude. The goal is to be mindful of your surroundings, appreciative and at peace. Simple to say, but a tough goal to accomplish, but one that can be had without any special preparation, equipment, or health or financial commitment. Learn to truly breathe. Your breath is one area of your life in which you have control. Simply breathe and focus only on your breath. As you relax, you are now ready to seize the day.

Miracle: Is Grief "Miracle Worthy"?

Seeing, hearing, feeling, are miracles, and each part and tag of me is a miracle.
—Walt Whitman, "Leaves of Grass"

Do you have hope that you are worthy of a *miracle*? Do you have faith and trust that you will feel normal again after loss, your personal miracle? Many of you will have the opportunity to put the very hard and difficult lessons of grief to good use, for both your betterment and to all with whom you come in contact. "Will I ever feel normal again?" This is the question we asked in Part 1. The short answer is a resounding YES. Of course, there are always exceptions to anything, but in time, if you are committed to doing healthy and realistic grief work you will feel the miracle of being normal again—the miracle that you can live again, be thankful again, love again. Maybe your miracle did not come in time to keep your loved one alive, but your miracle can come in time to make you love life again.

Nature: Get Your Nature "Tune-up"

Being in tune with the natural rhythms of nature we can learn a lot about ourselves. Wherever you live there are opportunities to enjoy nature. From a bird on a windowsill, to watching nature's finest at work in the wild. Seasonality is often the gateway to enjoying nature as well.

Walk, do not run. Get off the road and out on a walking path, notice your surroundings, place your hand in the sand or dirt, run your hand through the vegetation, listen to the birds, hear the sound of the wind rustling through the branches, notice real earth beneath your feet. What is the land telling you? What are the positive messages the land is teaching you? Nature unbridled. Drink it in, pure nature, pure heart, pure mind, clear conscience, pure bliss, even if fleeting and temporary. This is available to all, nothing is required other than to bring yourself and expect an upward attitude adjustment.

Patience

Are we there yet?

—every child on a road trip

Be patient with yourself. Self-growth is tender; it's holy ground. There's no greater investment.

—Stephen R. Covey

I ask you to cultivate patience. As the well-known humorous request imparts: "Lord, give me *patience*, AND GIVE IT TO ME NOW!" The bereaved I work with often tell me: "I want this over now!" or "How long does this last?" Patience is not our strong suit as humans. The Persian adage comforts us, "Yet this too, shall pass." But when we ask "How much longer?" a usual refrain is "I don't think I can go on like this for much longer." It is normal for grievers to be impatient with the speed of their progress and to become frustrated if they are still struggling with some tough days long after the death of a loved one. However, when pressed they will normally admit, that yes, they do see progress, it is just slower than they had thought. We have to be careful not to be derailed by a lack of patience, which whispers in our head that we are not grieving good enough or fast enough. Discouragement can set in when we do the small steps, have small successes but realize we still have sadness, and that our spirits have not fully lifted. Once again, trust the process and help yourself to an extra helping of patience. It is worth the wait.

Peace

When peace, like a river, attendeth my way,
When sorrows like sea billows roll;
Whatever my lot, Thou hast taught me to say,
"It is well, it is well with my soul."

—Horatio G. Spafford, "It Is Well with My Soul"

Nothing can bring you peace but yourself.

—Ralph Waldo Emerson, "Self-Reliance"

Peace can become a lens through which you see the world. Be it. Live it. Radiate it out. Peace is an inside job.

—Wayne Dyer

What would it mean to have peace in your life after loss? To enjoy inner calm and peace is even more elusive after loss. It is easy to focus on your loss causing additional stress, anxiety, and worry. To have peace of mind means you will need to look inward, calming your mind, and cultivating a growing acceptance of your loss over time. Is absolute peace possible? Possibly not, but the peace you need and deserve is available to you. *Be at peace.*

110

Perspective: Expect a Changing Perspective

The field cannot well be seen from within the field.

—Emerson

It is all about perspective—where you stand and where you elect to cast your gaze. After loss, it is natural to feel like you're driving in circles, not seeing where you are on the big map. I am reminded of being on a commercial airplane, on the runway with depressing heavy grey skies socked in overhead. I have been struck by the beauty soon after takeoff and flying for only a short few seconds, once the plane cut through the thick dark clouds, only to see brilliant blue skies and beautiful sunshine all around. Simply a change in perspective.

Whether you find yourself in a pit of despair, a muddy rut, or on a smooth highway, we have vastly different perspectives to approach our new future after loss. As we progress on our road ahead, our perspective will change, and hopefully our view ahead will become sunnier.

Look at your life from a new perspective. Clear your mind, reset your attitude, and recalibrate your life.

Truths from the Road: the Gift of Perspective

"I looked after him twenty-four hours a day for three years, and I would do it again for another 100 years if I could."

"My mother gave me the gift of perspective," said a son. "She was a minimalist and she told me 'you can't take it with you' which at her final days helped me understand I was working too much and that I needed to take some time to put my life in perspective."

"My grief used to be so sharp, it is so much softer now."

Positivity: Ac-cent-tchu-ate the Positive

Are you a positive person? Is your glass half empty or half full? How has your loss affected your positive outlook on life? No matter your answer, you need to pack a strong dose of positivity with you on our road to renewal. You are hopeful for better things to be on your horizon, and by accentuating your positive outlook you will be able to envision better things happening.

111

Prayer and Meditation

Simply find a time daily that works for you and be still. Dare to slow down, breathe, and center yourself. Take time to give thanks and to ask God or your higher power for support through the day. Whether you find ten minutes or thirty minutes a day, or ten minutes in the morning and ten minutes before bedtime, try to calm yourself and look within and beyond for your inner strength. The amount of time spent in reflection is not important, it is the simple discipline of being in a receptive mode to recharge and re-center yourself daily that is the key.

Resilience

Resilience is sometimes described as the art of being able to get up off the mat after being knocked down. It takes courage to brush yourself off after being knocked down, and it takes courage to reenter the arena and to get into the game again. After loss we have to summon our inner resilience to give us a chance to fully cope. One woman reported after losing her husband after many years of marriage, "I'm a little scattered, but I've got pretty good fortitude. I'm pretty *resilient*." I am asking you to become a resilient griever and if you are reading this book, I expect you are already resilient. As a resilient griever you will have hope and will develop a positive attitude that something good can and will come out of your toughest loss—that you will experience personal growth.

Self-care and Wellness for the Soul

[Self-care] is not self-indulgence, it's self-preservation.

—Audrey Lorde

Self-care starts with your*self*. To be your best self, look inward as well as outward. You need to give yourself the gift of self-compassion, self-kindness—not in a selfish way, but to fill your emotional and spiritual tanks first, so you can be of use to others. The inward nourishing of your soul will sustain you. How do you feed your soul? Embrace the solitude that surrounds you, seek beauty, enjoy the restorative and refreshing gifts of nature, learn to visualize positive imagery in your daily life. Self-care is investing in yourself. Invest your time and money in anything that helps you grow: reading and libraries, classes and courses, community centers and gyms, and inspirational and spiritual activities. Practice the self-care areas mentioned in Part 2: DOING.

Service: Beautiful Healing

If you're feeling helpless, help someone.

—Morley, "Women of Hope"

To serve is beautiful, but only if it is done with joy and a whole heart and a free mind.

—Pearl S. Buck, *To My Daughters with Love*

The key to healing is to give, to help, to serve. Service to others does two things, it helps those around you, and more importantly it helps you. Studies have shown that those who give their time, talents, and money to help others gain health benefits of reduced stress and a reduced risk of depression. Serving those around you, often through volunteering, helps one's self-confidence, self-esteem and overall sense of purpose and meaning. Find ways to be of service to others in your everyday life, you will be amazed how it takes your mind off of your loss. I will always remember the lesson I learned from one of our hospice patients who suffered from Parkinson's disease, who told me, "When I am helping others, my hands no longer shake." Remember that service to others is an important healing agent for your grief journey.

Signs: Presence, Unseen but Real?

Usually "signs" are not this obvious. Do you believe in signs from an unseen presence? Sometimes they come announced in more ways than meet the eye. You may have entered a time and place in your life where physical signs are evident to you. Be aware of both the obvious and more subtle signs you encounter.

Working with end of life in hospice, it is common for those who are actively dying to begin to "transition," that is to start to see and talk to those who have passed before them. To see a welcoming face, a beckoning gesture from those in heaven is very comforting for both the patient and his or her family. Some say that they see a white light or that everyone is dressed in white, or they see a bright white tunnel or some equivalent. If we can accept that our loved ones who were dying can have a glimpse of an afterlife, why can't we, who are not dying, receive similar comforting signs from our deceased loved ones? I invite you to be open to sense a presence of your deceased loved one through dreams, visitations, or simple signs in your daily life.

Pay attention to possible signs you may receive and embrace them. Like tears, not everyone will have them, but if you do have a sign from your loved one it often can mean the world. Open your eyes and senses to possible signs from your loved one, maybe it is a visit from mourning doves, butterflies, or cardinals; a number frozen on your clock, or a message on your computer that has special meaning.

Making decisions is one of the hardest things grievers have to do without their loved ones. Some who are grieving report receiving advisory dreams where the loved one helps validate an upcoming or recently made decision. One woman told me she woke up one night, to see her husband clearly on the ceiling with a "pleasant comforting smile." This gave her peace and affirmed her belief that he is happily in heaven. Others have been comforted by hearing their name sweetly called, and another woman said, "I just needed a sign that my husband is all right, that he is OK. I received the message, the vision, that he is with his mama, standing in beautiful green grass with a perfect blue sky. He would have loved that image." The understanding and acceptance of the presence of signs from a deceased loved one is growing daily within mainstream religions and society.

Paul McCartney recently explained the inspiration behind the writing of "Let It Be" to James Corden on the "Carpool Karaoke" piece that aired in 2019. McCartney recounted that his mother, named Mary, had died of cancer when he was age 14: "I had a dream in the sixties where my mum who died came to me in a dream and was reassuring me, saying: 'It's gonna be OK. Just let it be...'" McCartney leaves any reference to the Virgin Mary to one's own interpretation.

Truths from the Road: Signs, Sensing the Presence of your Loved One

"Every morning I have coffee and breakfast with [Mom] and we talk and talk. This is what we did when she was physically here. I am just keeping our relationship alive."

"I keep finding coins on the kitchen floor, and no one's been here. I like to think it is him."

"I hear him sometimes in the house saying to me, 'Now what are you doing?'"

"I feel close to my wife in the kitchen. She was a good cook and loved to be in the kitchen. I love to be in the kitchen to feel near her."

Seeking Comfort

"The urn brings me comfort and when I am in the room with the picture of my grandmother and her urn, I feel close to her."

"I had a vision after my mother died that she was guiding me around the giant potholes in the road."

"I love seeing my wife's robe on the back of the door."

Giving Guidance

"The words of my mother came to me in a dream to stop what I'm doing and start a career in nursing. That is what I am going to do."

"Words from my husband came to me telling me it is all going to be alright, and to make the most of this life."

Solitude: From Loneliness to Solitude

In solitude, where we are least alone.

—Lord Byron

Inside myself is a place where I live all alone and that's where you renew your springs that never dry up.

—Pearl S. Buck

Overcoming loneliness is the single most difficult task grievers face after loss. Loneliness is a hard journey to endure, and tough to master. Spending time alone can be very challenging, and for many it may be the first time in their lives that they spent a night alone. Coming home to an empty house is daunting. With it come the deafening sounds of silence and the imagined sounds of loved ones in the house. "I am just so lonely at night," said one man, "that's when I really miss her." When we learn to be comfortable alone, then we may see some of the beauty and merits of solitude.

The art of solitude is a worthy discipline to strive for and one in which to aspire. One woman told me after her loss, "I now realize how alone I am, weekends and holidays my friends are with their families, and since I do not have any family anymore, I am an orphan." One bereaved woman took comfort from the 2013 movie, *Our Souls at Night*, with Robert Redford and Jane Fonda, which depicted the unique way they combatted loneliness.

Trust

Trust that still, small voice that says, "This might work and I'll try it."

—Diane Mariechild

Loss can leave you on unstable ground, doubting your faith and your ability to cope. Don't let this happen. Trust can be elusive, and it is difficult to rally after loss, but this is precisely the time to make a concerted effort to get in touch with your inner trust. Merriam-Webster defines trust as "to hope or expect confidently" and it is important that you trust with confidence that you will move beyond your loss to healing. You will get your joy back; you will begin to feel normal again. Your trust will build as you take steps to move forward with your life. Open your heart, trust the process, and *trust yourself.*

Vulnerability: Your Secret Inner Strength

Vulnerability is the birthplace of innovation, creativity, and change.
—Brené Brown

Embrace vulnerability. Losing a loved one makes us vulnerable in many ways and our vulnerability is often revealed to us on our journey to healing. Being vulnerable is what makes us fully alive and can be considered our greatest strength. Make a pledge to yourself not to run away from vulnerability as you rebound from loss. We cannot insulate ourselves from the dangers and fears of this world. To love and to have lost, is the ultimate layer of vulnerability that grief bestows upon us. If we resist the risk to be vulnerable again in the future, we run the even greater risk of unhealthy roadblocks on our road to renewal.

BEING: The Road to Emotional Transformation

Our greatest foes, and whom we most chiefly combat, are within.
—Miguel de Cervantes

Time for an Emotional Tune-up?

We have a need to feel emotion. It is sometimes stated that "feeling is healing" which is the emotional equivalent of the physical "no pain, no gain" mantra. One man said, "I cry inside; I have to be a man and not show it." *Catharsis* is the Greek word for "cleansing." Can we cleanse our negative emotions? Perhaps not completely, but hopefully we can be aware of and DECREASE harmful and toxic emotions.

BEING: Decrease— Unpacking Negative Emotions

In alphabetical order, the following are negative emotions that, perhaps, you can unpack and decrease or leave behind at this time.

Anger: Anger Is Not a Four-Letter Word

Anger gets a bad rap. We think of it as a defect in our character or a four-letter word. Anger is real and natural and should be understood, not suppressed. It is not healthy to live with anger long term, but anger is very much part of the grieving process, and it is important to identify it and learn to manage it.

Anger, where is it coming from? Not all who have lost have anger, but many of you do. The bottom line simply is "my loved one is not here with me and that makes me mad." For good reason, the bereaved often feels cheated, that this death came out of nowhere. Sometimes anger is directed at God. Other times anger is directed at the medical community which either missed a diagnosis completely or did not find it early enough to help with treatment. One man stated: "I was promised that my wife had six months to live and she died in three weeks. I feel robbed." Others are angry with their loved ones, that they were stubborn or in denial or hid their condition for too long, not wanting to face bad news.

What can we do about it? If you are angry with God, let God know. If you are a believer, God already knows anyway. Pray that you can accept this loss without knowing the "whys" of life. Some may threaten to sue medical practitioners. If you feel you have been wronged in the diagnosis and treatment process or in an accident or crime involving other parties, by all means voice your concerns or complaints to the appropriate authorities.

To grow, that is to bear more fruit, you will need to prune bitterness out of your life, so you will be able to bear more fruit as you move from hurting to healing. This is your season of pruning. What will you prune?

My concern is you. You don't have to like the outcome of your loss, but to carry the additional burden of anger on top of your great loss can come with great emotional cost. If your anger continues to linger, talk with a professional or close confidant to help you release your anger, which will be absolutely key in your journey to healing.

ASK YOURSELF: Is this an area I need to decrease, to unpack? Y/N

BEING: From Anger to Peace and Contentment

Anxiety, Fear, and Worry: The Trifecta of Paralysis

Nothing diminishes anxiety faster than action.
—Walter Anderson

No one ever told me that grief felt so like fear.
—C. S. Lewis

Do not anticipate trouble, or worry about what may never happen. Keep in the sunlight.
—Benjamin Franklin

Are you here? Are you at the intersection of Anxiety, Fear, and Worry? If so, do not be alarmed as this too is perfectly normal. It is common to experience anxiety after loss, with the companions of fear and worry right behind. Knowing this is normal can be helpful as you identify these emotions and learn to adjust to your new reality. This is your challenge on your road ahead.

As stated earlier, death changes everything, so naturally expect to deal with heightened emotions and feelings. Anxiety is defined by Merriam-Webster as "a feeling of worry, nervousness, or unease, typically about an imminent event or something with an uncertain outcome." At the root of anxiety is fear—fear of something specific or general in nature, or fear of the future. Do not be surprised if you experience physical symptoms, such as headaches, nausea, and shortness of breath, which accompany your emotional anxiety. Death also confronts us with our own mortality for a seemingly double whammy.

ASK YOURSELF: Is this an area I need to decrease, to unpack? Y/N

BEING: From Anxiety, Fear, and Worry to Calmness and Serenity

Apathy: Finding a Path Beyond "Whatever"

Apathy is a sort of living oblivion.

—Horace Greeley

Apathy is one more road barrier to your well-being. You may experience a lack of interest, enthusiasm, or concern. If apathy is defined as "without feeling" then apathy has to be recognized as a significant barrier to overcome on the road to wellness after loss. With loss, often comes numbness and lack of energy combined with a loss of direction. Grievers will say, particularly in the early days, they have no interest in things that had interested them before, and nothing seems appealing or interesting and that they are sleepwalking through life. One overarching theme is that there is a pessimism about the future. The disinterest in life is compounded by the exhaustion and fatigue of grief; grief is absolutely draining. The challenge of moving beyond apathy, is simply getting engaged in your life again by the baby steps outlined in DOING and in this section on BEING.

ASK YOURSELF: Is this an area I need to decrease, to unpack? Y/N

BEING: From Apathy to Interest and Passion

Guilt and Survivor Guilt: Not Guilty

We were together—all else has long been forgotten by me.

—Walt Whitman, "Leaves of Grass"

I love this quotation by Walt Whitman, which to me means, I spent my entire life with my loved one and we shared everything. The one important thing was "we were together" and the rest are details. As we move further from the death of a loved one, we may begin to forget certain characteristics of our special person, and this can be terribly unsettling, and it can bring with it a tidal wave of guilt. You may think this person was central to my life and now I can't remember how he or she looked, or the sound of his or her voice. Don't be surprised if this happens to you, even if you have made every effort to safeguard the memory of your loved one through photos, videos, writings, and other mementos.

Don't be surprised, if you find yourself over time, forgetting about your loved one for a period of time, several hours or even a full day. Over time you may forget the birthday, or the anniversary of the death, or the anniversary of the diagnosis or any other important milestones in your life together. And when you do, you will no doubt feel guilty. You are human. It is normal and natural to sometimes forget even important dates, but rest assured the memory of your loved one is well alive inside of you.

Previously in this book we noted that after loss it is common to have guilt over the "shoulda, woulda, couldas" as you review your relationship with your loved one. The paradox is that those who were the most attentive and gave the most to their loved one seem to carry this guilt with them even more. Now is the time to let this guilt go. Your loved one knew you loved him or her and none of us are perfect. End of story. Many grievers also have guilt from decisions they were required to make at the end of life for their loved one. Your rule of thumb: if your decisions were made out of love and in the person's best interest, you are living in the no-guilt zone. Survivor guilt makes it harder to move forward. Some say the remedy for guilt is forgiveness. This also includes forgiving yourself. One man told me, "I feel guilty doing anything fun or enjoyable because she is not with me." As stated earlier, you owe it to you loved one's legacy to live a full life.

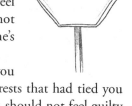

Living your full life means doing what is best for you and you may want to move beyond some of the interests that had tied you together with your loved one. That is normal and you should not feel guilty to chart a new course because of your changed circumstances.

ASK YOURSELF: Is this an area I need to decrease, to unpack? Y/N

BEING: From Guilt to Innocence and Goodness

Denial and Pride: When to Ask for Help?

No man is an island, entire of itself; every man is a piece of the continent.
—John Donne

Dust are our frames; and, gilded dust, our pride.
—Alfred, Lord Tennyson

Denial and pride can be roadblocks on the road to healing and renewal after loss. In our initial grieving we can view denial as a gift. Denial helps us adjust to our new reality after a numbing loss. Rather than drinking out of the high-pressure fire hose of loss, denial helps us cope with a slower stream of new information to process. On *your* road ahead please try to fully confront your loss, even if it is uncomfortable, and learn to leave denial behind.

Once you have left denial behind, you may be confronted with pride and self-reliance. You may be thinking "I can do this by myself" or "I don't need the help of anyone else." To ask for help for some grievers would indicate weakness or incompetence. The well-known phrase: "When lost, men don't ask for directions" comes to mind. This is pride speaking. This is the "Lone Ranger" concept. Your challenge on the road ahead is to shelve your pride and allow others to help you in this season of your life. Invite them in, no doubt there are those willing to help. You have nothing to lose but your pride. Do you need support? The answer is yes. Will you wish you had asked for support earlier? The answer is yes.

ASK YOURSELF: Is this an area I need to decrease, to unpack? Y/N

BEING: From Pride to Humility

Regret, Remorse, Shame: The Velcro Baggage

Forgive yourself for not having the foresight to know what seems so obvious in hindsight.

—Judy Belmont

Regret, remorse, and shame are the stickier Velcro pieces of emotional baggage that are harder to shed on your road ahead. Yet it is baggage we are not meant to carry.

Are you haunted by a decision? Hard places, tough choices. What happens if I was not able to honor a promise to keep my loved one home? What happens if I had to decide to end aggressive care for my loved one? What happens if I had to make decisions regarding the funeral or financial arrangements without input from my loved one? What happens if I was not able to force my loved one to see the doctor earlier? If any of these apply to you, then you may be haunted by a decision you made, or a decision you did not make (or did not make soon enough). If you have regret and wish you could go back to revisit your decision, please put yourself at peace knowing that you did the best you could under the circumstances. Just say no to 20/20 hindsight. You did not let your loved one down.

What happens when not all was said and done? If you were a caregiver for your loved one at the end of life, even with denial you may have known that time was limited. Even if you were grappling with a life-limiting diagnosis, you knew there was still hope—hope for a miracle. The last thing you or your loved one may have wanted to do is waste valuable time or risk fragile emotions to discuss those heavy but important topics. Often denial is the default mechanism and it is easier to "kick the can down the road," thinking there will be time for this later. When later comes, and perhaps "not all was said or done," consider the following takeaway: You did the best you could at the time under those circumstances and secondly, your loved one did the best he or she could have done at the time under those circumstances.

REMORSE: This is REGRET PLUS. This is regret on steroids, a deeper regret.

SHAME: Adding stigma to loss and regret.

ASK YOURSELF: Is this an area I need to decrease, to unpack? Y/N

BEING: From Regret, Remorse, and Shame to Contentment and Satisfaction

Sadness, Sorrow, Suffering, and Self-pity: The Four *S*'s of Emotional Pain

We were promised sufferings. They were part of the programme. We were even told, 'Blessed are they that mourn,' and I accepted it. I've got nothing that I hadn't bargained for. Of course it is different when the thing happens to oneself, not to others, and in reality, not imagination.

—C. S. Lewis, *A Grief Observed*

Believe it or not, we do have something to say about our emotions. It probably does not feel that way, but you are the owner of your emotions. Your owner's manual residing in your glove compartment is not personalized to you, so this is where you come in to create your unique road map. Are you ready to tackle the four *s*'s of emotional pain brought on by grief and loss? Here are the four *s*'s as defined by Merriam-Webster:

Sadness: causing or associated with grief or unhappiness

Sorrow: deep distress, sadness, or regret especially for the loss of someone or something loved

Suffering: to endure death, pain, or distress

Self-pity: a self-indulgent dwelling on one's own sorrows or misfortunes

The four *s*'s of emotional pain have a lesson to teach us and you may come to view some of these hard lessons as gifts. These lessons ensure you are fully awake and alive again. In the meantime, it may be wise to heed the words of a grieving woman who told me you have to "rip off your Three-P patch, your Pity Party Patch." If you are stuck in sadness, sorrow, suffering, or self-pity you will find strategies for coping and growth in the next section.

ASK YOURSELF: Is this an area I need to decrease, to unpack? Y/N

BEING: From Sadness, Suffering, Sorrow, and Self-pity to Contentment and Peace

Truths from the Road: Sadness, Anger, and Unforgiveness

"Money is now an issue."

"Who will look after me, I don't have anyone to look after me,"
said a man who had lovingly cared for his wife.

"I don't think I will ever forgive some of the things that
happened to me, but they don't bother me anymore, I just
never think about them."

"I'd be really pissed if I thought my husband was the only one
taken."

One man said that the first months after losing his partner he
was angry and sad, he now reports, "I am losing my sadness
and my anger. I'm working on replacing it with gratitude."

Part 4
DETOURS, GROWTH, AND DESTINATION—
The Hard and Beautiful Road

I can't go on. I'll go on.
　　　　　—Samuel Beckett, *The Unnamable*

Difficult roads often lead to beautiful
destinations. The best is yet to come
　　　　　　　　　　—Zig Ziglar

The pain passes but the beauty remains.
　　　　　　　—Pierre-Auguste Renoir

R U Stuck? Strategies for Getting Unstuck

If you are not moving forward, you may be stuck. What would a road trip be without some adversity? If you consider your loss to be your life's hardest journey, it seems reasonable to expect some rough roads ahead. To expect perfectly straight and smooth roads would not be honest or realistic.

Do you need to *look back to move forward*? Ask yourself if you need to do this at this time, if not, simply skip or skim through this section and continue to move forward. Don't give up, persevere and stay the course, rough roads are natural and normal, and can provide beautiful lessons.

Have You Stalled?

Your engine not turning over? In need of a jump-start? It is natural to stall out after a major loss, and not have the energy or inclination to get up and get started again. One man told me, "My life is stalled." Another said, "I was doing really well for several months, then it hit me. I feel stalled."

Are You Stuck in Grief?

The 11th Commandment: Thou shall not be stuck. If you are truly stuck, be comforted knowing this is normal and natural on this road after loss. But being stuck is not home, we are meant to move through grief, and not be stuck in it. Remember, even if you are idling in a parking lot for too long, you are in danger of running out of gas. The following are some tips and suggestions to help get you moving down the road again.

Speaking Your Truth Shall Set You Free

Sometimes we are stuck in grief because we have not been speaking the

124

truth to our family and friends, and possibly not even to ourselves. What truths are we talking about? It could be your true feelings about what happened during your loved one's end-of-life process. It could be your true feelings on how you have been personally treated. It is not uncommon to hear grievers say that they feel they have been "avoided" by those they know or that their loss has been "discounted" by friends and family. One woman shared, "I feel invisible and I don't think my loss has been fully validated by others." Another said, "I'm hurt and mad that my brother and sister-in-law can't even call me after losing my husband of forty-one years."

Talk it out, let those around you know how you feel, but try to speak from the vantage point of love rather than anger. Inform your family and friends that you owe it to them, as well as to yourself, not to keep quiet by bottling up emotions but to let them know what is on your heart. This is being true to yourself. Truth is always the best policy. Speaking the truth will give you a sense of normalcy and that will serve as an important step forward in restoring order out of the chaos that loss brings.

When All Was Not Said and Done

At the end of life, it is common that all was not said and done regarding the wishes of a loved one. Since the focus was on the "battle" to keep a loved one alive, sometimes these conversations did not happen. It is a gift if you were able to have "the talk" or "the conversation" and you knew exactly what your loved one's wishes were, but that is often not the case. Connecting the dots, you will need to remember that you did your best without input from your loved one, and it is important not to have guilt or regret from tough decisions that you may have had to make. You were no doubt focused on hope, and talk of other outcomes seemed to negate your efforts while hope was still on the table.

For many grievers, it seems almost disloyal to bring up death and what will happen afterwards. This conversation can be the most taboo of all, it certainly is harder and more uncomfortable than giving the "birds and bees" talk to children or discussing other difficult topics. When the tough decision had to be made, such as taking your loved one off a ventilator, ending dialysis, disabling a defibrillator, or moving to a nursing home or hospice house, second guessing is common. Put yourself in the shoes of your loved one that you lost, what would you have wanted for yourself? Would you be critical of decisions made? You made the best decision, based on the information, resources, and your physical and emotional condition at the time.

Your litmus test for decision making: if done out of love, you are good to go. Being gentle on yourself is easier said than done. Your homework is to work daily on giving yourself grace to let go of any guilt or regret you have regarding the decisions you were required to make.

Truths from the Road: Feeling Stuck

"I am stuck, I just need to know the next step."

"I can't see my way to the future."

"I am just keeping busy, worrying and angry about my situation, upset that this is not me to be like this. I just want to feel joy again."

"I am stuck in neutral; I just can't get in gear."

ROAD SCHOLAR ASSIGNMENT: What Are Your Roadblocks?

Identify three roadblocks, or potential roadblocks, that are stopping you from moving forward.

1. _____

2. _____

3. _____

Additional Comments?

_____

_____

_____

_____

_____

_____

_____

_____

Truths from the Road:
Is my ETA wrong?

"I cried and did my grieving for the first forty-eight hours. I am fine now." Same person, update weeks later: "I am surprised how I can't quite feel myself."

"What's wrong with me, I thought I would be over this in a couple of weeks."

"I have been struck by the permanence of the loss."

"I was shocked when I met a person who had lost their loved one over two years ago and is still grieving. Clearly, I thought this will not be me. I think it might be."

Rearview Mirror

We look at the present through a rearview mirror. We march backwards into the future.

—Marshall McLuhan

I have a really small rear-view mirror in my life. I look at the rear-view mirror for memories and learning experiences, but I've got a big front windshield I'm looking at right now.

—Pat Croce

Just as the inscription on a car side-view mirrors reads, "Objects may be closer than they appear" so too with your grief and healing. Instead of objects, think obstacles. Your obstacles or barriers to recovery may not only be closer, but probably are larger and more 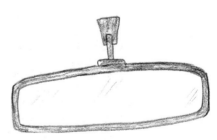 important than they appear. It is only a matter of perspective. Just as the mirror warns, so, too, your *fear, guilt,* and *regret* may be much closer or more important than they appear. Embrace any of these challenging obstacles or barriers you may be feeling and place them firmly in your rearview mirror.

Be gentle on yourself and continue forward with baby steps. As you move forward, remember your windshield is much larger than your rearview and side mirrors for a reason—your future well-being is more important than any issues of the past.

MILEPOST TIP: Why Not Enjoy a "Full" Filling Station Break?

How often do you stop to simply fill yourself up with positive comforting moments and experiences? Take a short break to enjoy the moment that is here. Enjoy the beauty of the sun coming in through your window, the sound of birds outside, or just breathe in some fresh air. Take a moment to fill yourself up with thankfulness or cast your eye on an object of beauty or your ear on a beautiful piece of music. *Come in empty, and fill yourself up.*

Can I Get a Lifeline?

Sometimes we are stuck and those closest to us are not able to throw us a lifeline. Sometimes those closest to us have no idea how to be around a person who is grieving. Sometimes we get the impression that our grief to others feels like a disease, that they might "catch our grief" from us. One woman stated when she finally asked a good friend why she hadn't called, she said, "'Oh, I didn't want to bother you' and I said I have no one to bother me."

In light of truth telling, let those in your inner circle clearly know your needs. Tell them in advance that you may or probably will cry. You can say, "I may cry, but don't worry, I'll pull it together and be OK, just give me a minute." Also, the bereaved tell me that they want their family and friends to know the following: "Don't give up on me." "Keep checking in, even if just for a few minutes, it's important to me." "Please bother me, I want to be bothered." "Please don't avoid me, I promise this won't last forever." "I need to say his name, and I want you to say his name."

Truths from the Road: Hard Place Observations

"I do my best crying in the car. I call it my Griefmobile."

"She was my best friend and we did everything together. Nothing special, we would go together to Home Depot to look for things to do to our house and yard."

128

Hitting the Invisible Grief Wall

Expect to hit an invisible "grief wall" and even a secondary grief wall once you thought you were making great progress. Or expect to feel blocked. Writers have a term for it, *writer's block,* when the creative juices dry up and writers find themselves stuck on a blank page, not able to move forward. So there certainly is no shame, to have "griever's block" and find yourself stuck. Grievers block can hit at any time, even after a period of seeming normalcy.

Beware the Mirage Effect

Just as your destination to healing seems to come into focus, it can just as quickly evaporate. Have you ever noticed driving on a highway on a hot summer day the road ahead appears wet, perhaps even a pool of water gathers, but the closer you get this body of water disappears? Making progress on your Destination Road can appear as a mirage, with healing just out of reach. This is normal.

No Parking Zone: Just Passing Through

On the road ahead you will no doubt travel through the rough grief neighborhoods of Shock, Numbness, and Hopelessness. DO NOT PARK HERE, just keep passing through. While we may be tempted to put down roots, we are not meant to stay in these neighborhoods. Do not unpack your bags here. No extended stays please. This is not your home.

Back to the Future Department

Do you need to go back to review and address any outstanding issues over the death of your loved one? We are not meant to be stuck by something that did or did not get done in the past.

Journal Thoughts _____

_____

_____

_____

_____

_____

_____

_____

ROAD SCHOLAR ASSIGNMENT: Feeling Stuck?

Consider completing one or more of the following exercises.

Lossography: Write a timeline in your notebook and list from your earliest memory all the losses in your life, such as, the loss of a pet, relationship, job, or loved one. If you have a loss from your past that you have not had the opportunity to grieve or complete grieving, this would be a good time to help you get unstuck. Remember, completing is not forgetting.

A Relationship Line Chart: In your notebook, draw a single line with year-date markers, with positive life events on top and negative life events below the line for the key people in your life. Ideally, for your personal growth you will learn to focus more on the positive side of the ledger moving forward.

Unstuck Letter: Finally, write an "unstuck letter" to your loved one, or to God, emphasizing the following: I forgive, I apologize, and I want you to know. In addition, consider writing this letter from your loved one to you, especially if there is something you always wanted to hear from your loved one.

Roadblock Ahead: Expect Detours

Every path has a puddle.

—George Herbert

Stop worrying about the potholes in the road and enjoy the journey.

—Babs Hoffman

My teacher used to tell us that to think is to meander from highway to byway, and from byway into alleyway, till we come to a dead end. Stopped dead in our alley, we think what a feat it would be to get out. That is when we look for the gate to the meadows beyond.

—Antonio Machado, *Juan de Mairena*

We are all under construction. We are building this road as we drive. Delays and detours will certainly be an expected part of your road ahead. On your road to renewal after loss, you will no doubt encounter roadblocks—roadblocks to feeling normal, roadblocks to joy and happiness, and roadblocks to your healing and recovery. *Identify which of the following detours you may need to address as your move forward.* This takes time and energy, which may be in short supply. Embrace the journey.

DETOUR STRATEGY #1:
Recognizing that You Are Stuck

First, you have to *know* that you're stuck. Admit to yourself that you are stuck. You have plenty of company as we all get stuck in life, especially if you lose the go-to person in your life. The grievers I work with often want to know "Am I going crazy?" "Is this normal?" "What's happening to me?" Combatting denial and recognizing that you are stuck is an important first step to healing.

DETOUR STRATEGY #2:
Got Change? Making
Peace with Change

It's only after you've stepped outside your comfort zone that you begin to change, grow, and transform.

—Roy T. Bennett, *The Light in the Heart*

Whether we like it or not, change is on the horizon. Our circumstances, in fact our entire world, has changed as a result of loss. The Greek philosopher Heroclitus professed that the only constant is change. With the death of your go-to person, this seems like change on steroids. So how do you adapt to your changed world? Let's look at some positives of change: the possibility of discovering your inner strength, your inner creativity, your inner resiliency, your inner stick-to-itiveness. We need to be open to change, because we can't resist it—it is already here. I am hopeful that you will poke your head out of your silo of change. Look around you, see what the big world has to offer. Share what you have to offer the world.

DETOUR STRATEGY #3:
Decisions, Decisions,
Why Can't I Decide?

Once you make a decision, the universe conspires to make it happen.

—Ralph Waldo Emerson

Warning, Fog Ahead. An inconvenient truth of grief is that important decisions often have to be made, sometimes quickly, but without your normal support in place. This may be the first time in your life that you are called to make major decisions, but with the handicap of not possessing your usual energy, while in the throes of "grief brain," and without your usual sounding board, your go-to loved one. One woman said, "Making decisions is the single hardest thing for me since losing John." So how do you navigate decision-making with one hand tied behind your back? Proceed slowly and allow yourself the grace to make decisions at your pace, not at the pace of others. Sometimes the best decision is to give yourself more time to decide.

DETOUR STRATEGY #4:
Fear and Risk, Growth Opportunity?

I've been absolutely terrified every moment of my life—and I've never let it keep me from doing a single thing I wanted to do.
—Georgia O'Keefe

You gain strength, courage and confidence by every experience in which you really stop to look fear in the face. You are able to say to yourself, "I have lived through this horror. I can take the next thing that comes along." You must do the thing you think you cannot do.
—Eleanor Roosevelt

We all need risk in our lives. Not unbridled risk, but risk balanced with thoughtful reflection. What then is holding us back from putting ourselves out there, getting out of our comfort zone? It is the powerful four-letter word, FEAR. Two questions to consider: What would I do if I had no fear? What would I do if I could not fail? To conquer fear, we have to *know* it and *own* it—not let fear own us. Taking a risk and getting out of one's comfort zone is difficult. Let this be gentle encouragement that when the time is right for you to let go of fear and step out with faith and trust that you will be fine in taking a step forward.

Journal Thoughts _____

_____

_____

_____

_____

_____

_____

ROAD SCHOLAR ASSIGNMENT: What Is Your Risk Profile?

List three risks you have taken in the *past*, and list three risks you may consider taking *now* on your road forward.

THE PAST	THE FUTURE
1. _____	1. _____
2. _____	2. _____
3. _____	3. _____

Additional Comments?

_____

_____

_____

_____

_____

_____

_____

_____

_____

_____

Truths from the Road: Fear

"I am fearful that I am going to lose someone else."

"I am fearful that I will die alone. Who is going to take care of me?"

"I fear illness more than death, death ends it."

"What will happen to me if something bad happens, who will be there for me?"

DETOUR STRATEGY #5:
We Are Family—Statement or Question?

Death brings out the best and worst in people, and nowhere is this truer than in families. Sometimes families are brought closer together after a death, and in other situations families that already had been in a tenuous situation before the death, can fall by the wayside.

- **The good:** "I was pleasantly surprised that my siblings, and particularly my brother, all rallied together to support each other after Dad's death." Another said, "We have become closer due to the loss and that helped us grow out of our estrangement and now we are becoming friends again as well as sisters." One man reported after the loss of his partner, "I have an improved relationship with his family. I now speak to them weekly and it is very satisfying, to come full circle. I was able to fill in missing details which helped bridge the gap that had been between them." A woman was comforted by a sister-in-law, "You weren't just married to my brother, you were married to our entire family."

- **The sad:** "My mother was the matriarch of the family, and now that she is gone, my siblings and their families don't get together like we used to, that's so sad to me."

- **The bad:** "I inherited the farm from my aunt, now I have the entire family mad at me." Perhaps the family home needs to be sold or possessions divided up, and some family members are perceived to benefit more than others, placing additional strain on family relations. The strategy is to address your concerns or reasons in a loving and supportive manner and try to take the high road of giving your fair share and then some so you will feel peace and have healing moving forward.

- **Blended families:** When all is well, it is beautiful to see all hearts connected and all labels taken away, just sharing love for the one who died. One man said about his family, "There is no 'step' in our family, all are our children regardless of who gave birth." A woman commented, "We have his, mine, and ours and it all works." For others in blended families, death can separate and isolate an individual from the family he or she may have been part of for decades, such as a stepparent no longer having access to children or grandchildren anymore, or at least not to the level previously experienced. Similar situations are a concern, and simply put, present another loss compounded on top of the death.

- **Estranged and "toxic" family members:** Some grievers report one or more family members as "no shows" or report those with a self-interested or critical spirit. Unhelpful comments, such as "just get over it" or "we need to clear the house now," may mean that this is the time to guard your heart and accept that others in your life will be operating with differing motives and timetables. One woman had enough of a toxic family member saying, "I won't give him free rent in my brain anymore."

If conflict appears on the horizon, and your reasonable and conciliatory efforts were rebuffed, then this may be the time to move forward with or without everyone on board. Perhaps this is the time to find your *chosen* family.

Exits Ahead: What Is Your Exit Strategy?

Look on every exit being an entry somewhere else.

—Tom Stoppard, *Rosencrantz and Guildenstern Are Dead*

At your discretion, please consider taking one of the following exits for a "tune-up" or for additional work on your grief. Your exit strategy is to *exit grief* on your own terms. If your *Service Now* warning light comes on, respond to any of the relevant tune-up opportunities ahead and exit now for further help and attention.

Exit: What Is Your Flat Tire?

Is there a possible "flat tire" that has you stuck? List in your notebook anything that is challenging you now or that you will have to deal with in the near future. This may not be something major, but to you it is irritating and frustrating and a concern. For example, it could be something that your spouse or loved one normally was in charge of that now falls in your lap, such as paperwork, bill paying, mowing the lawn, cooking, or completing fix-it projects around the house. Or it could be situations with finances or family members that only arose because of your loss. These are all reminders of your loss, hence the FLAT TIRE. Identify your concern and address it. It is only a flat tire—know that you will be able to move forward soon.

Exit: What Now? Backslide Alert!

Expect on this journey for your internal warning light to go off, signaling time for a tune-up. It is highly probable that you will have some nagging grief issues return or maybe even be hit by a wave of grief, enough to stall you in your tracks. Many bereaved people tell me that in the initial weeks and months, they kept busy with all the essential tasks. First, there was communicating with so many people on the loss of their loved one. Then there was the planning of a memorial service, celebration of life, or gathering to honor their loved one, with relatives and friends in abundance. Then there was the business of grief, so much paperwork and dealing with banks, insurance, and trusts. Perhaps you said something like the following: "I kept my emotions in check" or "I was strong for my family" or "I had this grief thing under control. What is the big deal? It is not as bad as I thought" or "I felt good and productive."

Grievers often report that once they completed the half-dozen or so tasks that needed to be done and weathered the initial wave of grief, the full impact of their loss hit them. "Once I completed all my tasks, it hit me 'now what?'" NOW WHAT? "What the hell am I going to do with the rest of my life," a man stated after he had fulfilled his late wife's wishes to take their grandchildren to Disneyworld after her death. He did this dutifully, he organized the flights, hotels, and all of the activities, and they had a whale of a time. He was surprised to find an empty feeling on his return home. WHAT NOW?

Exit: Grief on Grief

Expect multiple losses. Sometimes the losses are just an accumulation of bad news, not all ending in death—from yourself dealing with your own health issues and "stuff" or your family and friends for whom you care deeply receiving bad news. We do not live in a bubble or vacuum. Working through grief, we are often rocked by these additional speed bumps of compounded grief, with the news of a close friend or family member who is suffering from a bout of adversity. Sometimes multiple losses come in short succession, one woman with multiple losses said, "I am a big ball of tears. I don't know who I am crying for." "Just as I seemed to be managing with my loss," said another, "the news of my best friend pushed me back downhill. It was like more grief piled on my other grief."

Exit: Expect Boomerang Grief

It comes back. With grief, it is not a one-and-done process. Some of the same themes of our healthy grieving that we thought we had worked through come back again. That's OK and absolutely normal. Sometimes it is an obvious trigger that sends the boomerang back, such as visiting the gravesite, but other times it comes out of the blue without any explanation. This is normal. If any of these themes arrive back to you, address them openly, greet them with a welcome that you have been expecting them, and then let them go again.

Exit: When the Second Year Is Hardest

Speaking with those whose loss is more distant, some reported that the second year after their loss was the most difficult for them. Sometimes those who make it through the first year were sleepwalking or simply numb and anesthetized throughout the entire calendar year. I often hear people say they are determined to make it through the first year and they hold on tight with white knuckles, but once the calendar turns over to the second year, the expectation of something magical happening is usually absent. The second year can be harder for some, as it may mean being fully awake (without anesthetic) to the reality of the loss and grief seems more real.

Exit: Grief Vortex?

Sometimes you may just need to wave the white flag and surrender. When hit by a grief vortex, the force of it just may be too powerful for you to immediately overcome. Put this book down until this storm passes, seek professional attention if needed, and simply ride the storm out, for it too will pass. If you are continually crying, not able to get out of bed or not willing to get out of the house, know that better days are still possible, and will come, but today is not that day. Once the "grief fever" breaks, make the most of the energy you have and pick up this book again.

Exit: Acceptance, Accepting the Past

The past is past. Remember, *yes*. Judge, *no*. Healthy grieving means remembering the past. Healthy grieving does not mean judging the past. Consider living now in the NO JUDGMENT ZONE. Over time, healthy grievers *choose to remember* the most positive aspects of the past, not judge what could have been, what should not have happened, or what could have happened. Acceptance of the past, both good and bad, is your road to personal growth.

Exit: Weigh Station, Oversized or Overweight Baggage?

On your road you will come to a weigh station to inspect the weight/baggage you are carrying. You may discover you are still carrying emotional baggage you had hoped earlier to leave behind. Is this true for you? Take time now to check for unwanted emotional baggage that you can shed now or in the near future. Remember, jettisoning emotional baggage is hard to do and perfection is not available to us, so it is better to shed some of your unwelcome baggage now, than cling to it all.

Road Closed Ahead? When Grief Is Complicated

Professional help is encouraged and may be essential.

All grief is complicated. Grief is a hard journey, but when it is compounded or complicated with additional personal issues, it can create a sense of hopelessness. Your grief may then seem unbearable to you. As this book is not meant to be a substitute for treatment or therapy, I recommend that you follow up with grief and mental health experts if you find yourself described in the following scenarios.

Complicated Grief Is Like Grief Quicksand

Complicated grief is like getting stuck in quicksand, *grief quicksand*. Any movement is difficult and moving forward seems impossible. Pulling out of complicated grief is hard work and requires perseverance as well as time, and it may require the assistance of professionals to help you become unstuck.

Journal Thoughts _____

_____

_____

_____

_____

_____

When Grief Is Complicated by Stigma and Shame

Grief can be complicated when the loss is compounded by stigma or shame. When the loss was in part caused by or brought on more quickly by what others view as self-indulgent behavior—alcohol or drug abuse, smoking, or death by overdose or suicide—grief is complicated. Grief is hard enough, but when stigma and shame are attached it adds an extra layer of complication.

When Grief Is Complicated by Lack of Acknowledgment or Understanding

Grief can be complicated when the loss is not legally acknowledged through marriage or a will and the griever is placed on the sidelines—frozen out of funeral planning and future financial affairs by the family. Grief is complicated when the loss cannot be publicly acknowledged, such as by a partner in an extramarital affair. Grief is complicated for one who is not recognized as a griever because his or her relationship with the deceased had changed, such as a former partner or spouse, who still grieves the loss. Grief is complicated when grievers find themselves misunderstood and not supported after their loss, especially if their ethnic, racial, cultural background, or identification as a member of the LGBTQIA+ community comes into play as an issue.

When Grief Is Complicated, Loss of a Child

Grief is complicated with the loss of a child. Parents know that it is not in the natural order of things to have their child die before themselves. Whether death comes through illness, accident, or suicide, the loss of a child can be a difficult and complicated road. Grief can be complicated for perinatal and neonatal deaths as such a loss can be discounted by society, since the child did not have the opportunity to leave a full mark on the world.

Hard Roads Can Teach Beautiful Lessons

From the dark end of the street to the bright side of the road
—Van Morrison, *"Bright Side of the Road"*

Nothing ever becomes real till it is experienced—Even a proverb is no proverb to you till your life has illustrated it.
—John Keats

Sometimes the most scenic roads in life are the detours you didn't mean to take.
—Angela N. Blount, *Once Upon an Ever After*

The Detour Makes the Journey

The unintentional joy and benefits of detours and exits are the beautiful lessons that your hard road ahead provides. Learn to embrace the detour and be on the lookout for the unexpected beauty that blooms in your midst.

Serendipity Ahead?

Serendipity is defined by Merriam-Webster as "finding valuable or agreeable things not sought for." After the loss you did not want, it is possible that you will "find valuable or agreeable things" moving forward. Look for these valuable and beautiful lessons in your present life.

Get Lost?

You may have found yourself unexpectedly off road and lost. Perhaps you took the "wilderness of grief" exit and *found yourself while lost*. This is the paradox of the hard road. Be open to learning beautiful lessons about yourself. Expect to "find" yourself while lost.

Put It in Neutral?

Sometimes doing nothing is the best option. It may be an invigorating detour for you. The joy of doing nothing is not to be overlooked. One lesson of the hard road is that you will need to recharge your batteries. The beauty is that you can now gain a perspective through introspection. Once you are recharged, you will be able to shift into drive and move forward.

Thank You and Goodbye

It is OK to say goodbye to the hard and unpleasant detours and exits on your road to healing. THANK them for helping teach you important life lessons and wave goodbye to them in your rearview mirror. GOODBYE.

Truths from the Road: Observations, Revisited

"Something is wrong with this picture," a father stated. "I have two pieces of paper in my hand, my son's birth certificate and my son's death certificate."

"I am so sad that I don't have my mother with me to choose my wedding dress and to be with me every step of the way."

Scenic Views from the Hard and Beautiful Road

SCENIC OVERLOOK: Miracle on the Horizon?

There are only two ways to live your life. One is as though nothing is a miracle. The other is as though everything is a miracle.

—Albert Einstein

Can you see your miracle waiting for you on the horizon? Are you able to believe that *everything is a miracle*? Are you able to say the following?

- It is a miracle I survived my loss.
- It is a miracle that I have hope and trust that I may one day feel normal again.
- It is a miracle that I am able to look forward to the future.
- No matter my place on the economic ladder, it is a miracle that I have life's most basic provisions. I have a roof over my head, running water, and a bed in which to sleep.
- It is a miracle that I am alive, and even if my physical or mental faculties have been diminished, I still can function in this world. I still can contribute. I still can have meaning and purpose. *A miracle.*

SCENIC OVERLOOK: Glimpse of Heaven

Someday I'll wish upon a star. And wake up where the clouds are far behind me.

— E. Y. Harburg and Harold Arlen, "Over the Rainbow"

From this marvelous overlook, the vista is endless, in fact it is so endless it reminds us of eternity—the eternity we carry within us. If you are lucky enough, expect to be surprised by glimpses of heaven on the road ahead that give you encouragement for healing. Glimpses of heaven are within your reach, little foretastes of your future earthly destination and beyond.

Truths from the Road: My Scenic Overlook

"My mother and I would sit out on the swing and listen to the birds whistle. Now when I sit in the swing and hear the birds whistle, I think of my mother and smile."

"Travelling from Colorado early in the morning we followed the sunrise and witnessed the majesty of an unblocked view of a gorgeous sunrise. I stopped and was beautifully surprised to find monarch butterflies everywhere as we accidentally chanced on a way station for these monarch butterflies on their way to hibernation. I thought about Earl."

ROAD SCHOLAR ASSIGNMENT: Do You Have a Scenic View?

Consider a scenic overlook. Take a break from the hard road to look around, to see beyond your circumstances and notice the beauty of the world that surrounds you. Take in the scenic reminder that life can be awesome if we are able to look well beyond the horizon, beyond the storm clouds of grief and fear, so that we can see clearly. What is your view from the road? *In your notebook, describe your scenic view.*

ROAD SCHOLAR ASSIGNMENT: What Lesson Has the Hard and Beautiful Road Taught You?

The Hard and Beautiful Road has taught me the lesson of . . .

_____

_____

_____

Truths from the Road: What has grief taught you?

"To seize the day. I know too many people who put off doing something thinking they had time later, and they didn't."

One man who had been married thirty-eight years said, "I learned to sew on a button, and it is still on, thanks to YouTube videos."

A daughter who cleared out the contents of her parents' home, stated "it has made me let go of material things."

The Road to Growth: The Drive Beyond

Every blade of grass has its Angel that bends over it and whispers, "Grow, grow."

—The Talmud

There's no GROWTH without change. No CHANGE without loss. No LOSS without grief. No GRIEF without pain.

—Rick Warren

For a seed to achieve its greatest expression, it must come completely undone.
The shell cracks, its insides come out and everything changes.
To someone who doesn't understand growth, it would look like complete destruction.

—Marcel Proust

The fatal metaphor of progress, which means leaving things behind us, has utterly obscured the real idea of growth, which means leaving things inside us.

—G. K. Chesterton

Growth itself contains the germ of happiness.

—Pearl S. Buck, *To My Daughters, With Love*

You are on the road to growth. Moving from "hanging on by my finger-nails" and "survival" to "doing OK" and "getting by" has been a lofty goal and a sign of progress for most grievers. Sometimes grievers want more, and after a length of time many report "feeling better every day" and may be knocking on the "pretty good" or "even better than I expected" door. Welcome realistic challenges and opportunities for growth that can help you build momentum and self-confidence. Growth can come in bunches, it can come in spurts, or come slowly one mile marker at a time.

The Gift of Growth

There is a such a beautiful gift that comes tied to your loss. You have received life's wake-up call, that our mortality is both crushing and stunningly beautiful. It is a clarion call to live *now*. Through your loss, your heart has been specially trained, and I believe God does not want anyone to waste that hurt. The gift of growth might mean for you to be able to be more compassionate and to reach out to others who have experienced loss. You will learn in time to be a good steward of this gift, to grow as a person, and to be of service to others, which will provide meaning and purpose to your life. You are now specially equipped to value life and "the moment," living in the now, no longer taking life for granted, that is, to feel fully alive since you have fully tasted both joy and sorrow. Prepare to be "surprised by joy" on this road ahead.

Growth: Your Reason and Season to Grow

There is ripe fruit over your head.
—Henry David Thoreau

We come from the earth, we return to the earth, and in between we garden.
—Alfred Austin

An optimistic gardener is one who believes that whatever goes down must come up.
—Leslie Hall

Why not go out on a limb? That's where the fruit is.
—Mark Twain

Bloom where you are planted.
—Saint Francis de Sales

In Part 1, it was revealed that growing to give is the secret of healing. This is your season to grow, but to grow—that is, to bear more fruit—you will need to learn to prune any bitterness out of your life. This will allow you to be able to bear more fruit, as you move from hurt to healed. This is your season of pruning. *What will you prune?*

Growth: The Empathy Bridge

Like a bridge over troubled water.

—Paul Simon, "Bridge over Troubled Water"

After your loss you no doubt desired empathy, not pity, from others. You are learning the important lesson of empathy. As you grow from expressions of self-pity to empathy for others, you may find yourself becoming a "bridge" for others to help them over their troubled waters of loss. Empathy is a bridge to healing.

Empathy Road: What Do You Have to Offer?

Yourself. Your loss has uniquely prepared you with an extra dose of empathy. One woman told me, "I know I am more empathetic than I used to be." I am willing to bet you are more empathetic, too, so be quick to listen, support, and encourage others; be generous with both your time and encouragement; and do your best to be a good friend, coworker, or family member. Show your gratitude by letting the light from your gratitude lamp brighten the lives of those around you. Flexing your empathy muscles will help lighten the load of others and you will be blessed as you are a blessing. This is the gift of giving.

Growth and Your Evolving Grief

It's a happy life, but someone is missing. It's a happy life, and someone is missing.

—Elizabeth McCracken

People often say grief is an emotion that never goes away. It is true that we will always miss our loved ones, but it is also true that we can move forward and live productive and meaningful lives after loss. That does not diminish our love or loyalty to people who are no longer physically present in our lives. As we grow, our grief evolves. Grievers tell me their grief is constantly changing as the days, weeks, months, and years pass. I like to reframe this by saying that our loved ones are in our hearts forever, and gratitude, rather than grief, will occupy a greater share of our hearts.

Over time it is common for grievers to say that their burden of grief has lightened, that they are "getting stronger every day." The weight of grief is

still there but it is not as great as before. Even if the weight of our grief stays the same weight, our arms are strengthened and our shoulders and backs are broadened, which help us carry the load.

The Passage of Time and Growth

For time is the longest distance between two places.

—Tennessee Williams, *The Glass Menagerie*

Growth is often the byproduct of the passage of time. The adage that "time heals all wounds" is only partially true, it all depends on what you do with your time. Emotional healing is a long-term, ongoing process. Some who report that they are "getting better every day" often admit to still having rough hours in those days or a difficult day or two. The positive effect on those who report that they are getting better should not be underestimated. The getting-better mantra can serve as a self-fulfilling prophecy as it starts to seep in and is actualized by the griever.

Truths from the Road: After the Passage of Time

"It doesn't hurt like it did."

"It's getting easier to take a ride and not cry all the time."

"It's OK to laugh."

Six Months after Loss

"I have decided to no longer muscle through my grief. I have decided to no longer intellectualize my grief. I have decided to just live my life and pick up doing my normal things."

After One Year

"I came back alive."

"I need to exhale for a minute, sit down and search my heart. I haven't had a chance to grieve yet."

New Year's Resolution

"Today is the day to stop hanging on to my pain."

"Find one thing to smile about each day."

SCENIC OVERLOOK: Rainbow Deferred

One can enjoy a rainbow without necessarily forgetting the forces that made it.

—Mark Twain

Somewhere over the rainbow, bluebirds fly

—E. Y. Harburg and Harold Arlen, "Over the Rainbow"

For many who grieve, the storms of the early days and weeks do not produce rainbows right away. For most of us, we have to wait quite some time to see the rainbow created from the storms of our lives. But delayed rainbows are particularly beautiful. Be on the lookout for these delayed rainbows. Do you have a rainbow that is coming into view after the storm?

GROWTH AHEAD: Flipping Your Growth Switch

Don't go through life, grow through life.

—Eric Butterworth

Can we flip our internal growth switch to "on" to include acceptance and transformation? That would require us to be bold and to show courage—basically, audacious. I have been told by a number of grievers that they woke up one morning with an epiphany, a feeling that today is the day to start or stop a certain action. A change occurred and their growth switch flipped on. Sometimes this happens on a day of importance, such as an anniversary or the start of a new season. Here's to you preparing your own intellectual, emotional, and spiritual groundwork so that when that moment arrives, you, too, will be able to, without hesitation, flip your growth switch and be on your way to your new personal direction.

Expect Acceptance

Accept the past as past, without denying it or discarding it.

—Mitch Albom, *Tuesdays with Morrie*

It is a significant moment on your journey when you can point to being at peace with both yourself and your loss. This acceptance of your loss and changed circumstances is vital in your acceptance of your new personal life direction. Acceptance means living beyond perfection, to accept that the life you had is not available to you, and to be in acceptance of the life you have and are now creating. Acceptance is a gift, but the gift comes with the hard knocks and dents of life. I love the legacy story of acceptance relayed by a woman whose deceased husband said, "Why thank you, Jacob, I really needed my new car to have its first dent" after their young grandson accidentally christened grandpa's new car, his pride and joy, with a baseball bat. Acceptance is not easy, but it is necessary for our healing journey.

Expect Transformation

The call of death is a call of love. Death can be sweet if we answer it in the affirmative, if we accept it as one of the great eternal forms of life and transformation.
—Hermann Hesse

Is it audacious to be expectant of transformation? Why not, transformation is available and your loved one would be proud. Expect personal transformation, it may not feel like it is happening, or that it is in slow motion, but transformation is happening. Change is guaranteed, transformation is optional.

Fear of transformation is too real for many bereaved. "I do not want to be transformed," said one woman. "I do not want to lose my grief, if I lose my grief, I lose my grip on my loved one," said another. "I am happy here in my little grief corner of the world." True, but transformation happens, even in the most subtle ways. Perhaps grief has the power to transform us. Are we like the caterpillar, protected by its hard cover, that totally transforms itself to eventually emerge as a butterfly? Maybe the chrysalis or cocoon of grief allows us to take our time and eventually emerge transformed as a result of our loss.

SCENIC OVERVIEW: Your Growth Vista

Take a break and look back at how far you have traveled. It is OK to be overwhelmed with the view. Revel in the realization that you have moved forward in so many ways that you would never have thought possible—ways that are thoughtful and respectful, and surprising to yourself. *Enjoy the view* of just how far you have traveled. Progress is progress and needs to be celebrated. Honk your horn, pat yourself on the back. *Go ahead, no one is looking!*

Journal Thoughts _____

_____

_____

_____

_____

The Road to Legacy

Because I knew you I have been changed for good.
—Stephen L. Schwartz, "For Good" from *Wicked*

The hinges of love never rust
—inscription on Saint Luke's Hospice House memorial brick

I don't know what your destiny will be, but one thing I know: the only ones among you who will be really happy are those who have sought and found how to serve.
—Albert Schweitzer

You have two obligations regarding legacy. First, you owe it to the legacy of your loved one to lift up his or her memory after death by keeping that person alive in your heart. Second, you owe it to your loved one, to live your life to the fullest to honor the memory of the deceased person, thereby helping to create your own legacy.

- **Understanding the legacy of your loved one**

I believe the popular advice that we should give our children both *roots and wings* also applies to legacy. Your loved one has given you roots and wings. You have been shaped by your loved one and you are part of your loved one's legacy and that is *roots*. Your loved one is giving you *wings* to live life to the fullest after physically departing from this world. You have done the same and will expect your loved ones to have their wings once you depart this world.

- **You are the "designated legacy" representative**

  You owe it not only to yourself, but to your loved one, to make the most of the days you have remaining on this earth. You are the "designated legacy" representative, not only for yourself, but also for your loved one. If enjoying a moment of pleasure ushers in survivor-guilt thinking, try your best to put this aside. In a sense, you are charged with making this life count, as you are living for both yourself and your loved one. While you reach for a slice of "normal life" again, *smile* knowing that this is exactly what your loved one would want for you.

Truths from the Road: Stories of Remembrance

One man said sitting with photo and mementos: "This brings me half pain and half warm-hearted feeling of love and I like to do this."

"What I remember about my mother is that her kitchen was open twenty-four hours a day, and her heart was open twenty-four hours a day."

A woman had this to say about her husband, "He was a city boy who did not like the ocean or mountains, but he went there because it made me happy. He was happiest when I was happy."

Strategies for Honoring the Legacy of Your Loved One

Don't cry because it's over; smile because it happened.

—Ludwig Jacobowski

The following selections are meant to inspire you to find those areas of remembrance that honor the legacy of your loved one. Remembrance and legacy building are helpful in your healing journey.

- **Create a memorial**

  By the time you are reading this, you may already have had a funeral, memorial service, Celebration of Life, or gathering of family and friends to honor your loved one. Continuing to honor your loved one in any formal or informal memorial way is healthy and healing after loss. You may want to honor your loved one on a special day, the anniversary of the death or a birthday, or any day that is meaningful to you. There are absolutely unlimited ways, both small and large, to celebrate and honor the legacy of your loved one. Go online for additional ideas. The following are several ideas that grievers have said worked for them.

- Plant a tree, flowers, or shrubs
- Add a bench, memory stone, or statue to your garden
- Memorialize a park bench with a plaque
- Memorial jewelry
- Memorial tattoo
- Memorial shadowbox, scrapbook, or photo collage
- Quilt, blanket, or shirt made from your loved one's clothing
- Donate to a memorial garden
- Sponsor a scholarship or donate to a charity in honor of your loved one

- **You are a living monument**

  You are a living monument to the memory of your loved ones, honoring them, making them proud, by living your life to the fullest. You are on the road of monument building, moving from RIP "Rest in Peace" for your loved one, to RIP "Remembering in Peace" for you.

- **Cremation, now what?**

  As cremation has become the most popular form of disposition, many grievers have to decide what to do with the cremains. With the flexibility of cremation, that decision may be placed further down the road and not made immediately following the death. This can either be a healing opportunity or a source of stress. One woman told me that after the cremation of her husband, "I'm looking for a lower cost permanent interment of ashes, but I'm taking my time." Others are making plans to have the cremains of their loved one interred or scattered with their own at their death. One woman said, "I want him with me, that is where he would want to be. When I die we will have our ashes buried together."

- **Celebrate your celebration days**

  Be intentional to remember the important days you shared together. Make a plan in advance so you are not blindsided and find ways to celebrate in a meaningful manner. Embrace opportunities to celebrate special days and milestones as they will help you deal with loss.

- **Keep passions alive**

  Consider keeping the passions of your loved one alive, even if they are not fully your thing. It does not have to be full-blown involvement, even a symbolic nod to their interests or hobbies can be very important and therapeutic. If the activity was something you did together and you enjoyed it, consider keeping this going, even if you take a temporary break from it.

- **Remembrance travel**

  You may have plans to spread the cremains of your loved one in a special place or places that have meaning to you that require travel. Or you may want to, over time, retrace your steps and return to areas or places of importance to you and your loved one. This type of commemorative travel is a wonderful way to lift up your legacy together while on your road to healing. You may want to plan a connection vacation. Some bereaved will visit locations they had planned to visit together, but were not able to do so before the death. One woman mentioned that her husband always wanted to go on a cruise, and she hopes to go on a cruise in the future to honor him. If you are physically unable to go, consider having a trusted friend or family member help you with your legacy making. One bereaved woman wanted to honor her husband by having his cremains distributed in beautiful national parks because her husband was happiest in the great outdoors. Since she was not in a position to travel, a good friend was able to assist in honoring both her and her loved one through this meaningful act of kindness.

- **Remembrance through giving**

  It is common for the bereaved to make a time or financial donation to those nonprofit associations that have been meaningful to the family. Supporting a cause that was dear to your loved one's heart or joining the fight to find a cure or solution to the manner in which your loved one died, are all valuable to the healing process. Sometimes those with financial resources may donate funds for a scholarship in the name of their loved one. Small gestures, such as a family treated to a special dinner made possible by the funds left by the deceased, can be a great way to honor and pay tribute in a real way. One man told me he was making donations in honor of his partner, but he did not want to give to medical causes as they had in the past, but to honor his loved one through cultural offerings that would help benefit others. Honoring a legacy does not have to be based on the interests of the one who died, but rather according to the interests of the one who lives on.

- **Creating a family legacy project**

  Why not celebrate your loved one and your life together with a memory book or photo album? All it takes is a little time and effort, and don't say you lack creativity. No one can tell the story of your relationship better than you. What if I have limited energy and resources? That's OK, start small. Gather a few photos or keepsakes and place in a box, and over time you will have enough material to lay out for your memory book. It is better to begin now rather than to wait until the perfect time, because the perfect time never seems to arrive. What if I don't want to start because I am missing a photo, or can't find a special memento or keepsake? That's OK too, list what it is that you want to include on a sticky note and put in your memory book box to search for later. It won't take long before you have developed some momentum which will help you get it to the finish line. Remember you are not striving for perfection. Enlist others to help if you want, the more the merrier. You will be glad to have this memory book.

Truths from the Road: Honoring a Legacy

"This Christmas we all wore my grandmother's Christmas sweaters to honor her. It was great."

"My grandpa was a hat man; we all wore his hats at his celebration of life."

"I brought a box of my husband's bow ties to my nephew's wedding, and all of the men wore them in honor and celebration, it was wonderful."

"I'm working on a memorial wall in the house, to paint army green with his plaques from his years in the service."

SCENIC OVERLOOK: Taking a Sentimental Journey

Gonna take a sentimental journey . . . To renew old memories
—Benjamin Homer, Bud Green, Les Brown, "Sentimental Journey"

Taking the off-ramp for a scenic overlook is not only allowed, but is encouraged. It is OK to take a few minutes now, armed with memories of your loved one, to take a sentimental journey back in time. One patient I worked with wrote her own "Sentimental Journey" lyrics and put her song to music with the help of our music therapist. What is your sentimental journey?

Understanding Your Legacy: What Will Be Your Legacy?

If I knew I would die tomorrow, I would plant a tree today.

—Martin Luther

The meaning of life is to find your gift. The purpose of life is to give it away.

—Unknown

A Reason to Live: Finding Meaning and Purpose

We need something to live for. We all need a reason to get out of bed in the morning. After a loss, we are given the opportunity to look within ourselves and to review our purpose on Earth. What could our purpose be? If a world-changing purpose seems out of reach, perhaps our purpose may be solely to be thankful for the beauty and majesty of everyday life. Or to find an opportunity to smile, say a kind or encouraging word, or just be of help to another person—as often as our imperfect selves can muster.

What Will You Do with Your Dash?

For all that has been, Thanks. For all that will be, Yes.

—Dag Hammarskjöld

The two most important days in your life are the day you are born and the day you find out why.
—Unknown

You don't choose the day you enter the world and you don't choose the day you leave. It's what you do in between that makes all the difference.
—Anita Septimus

It's about the dash. It is what you will do with the rest of your life without your loved one physically by your side. It's what you do with your dash, the dash between the year you were born and the year you die, that makes all the difference.

154

What Will Be Your Legacy?

Start with the end in mind, ending well. We want our lives to end well. We all want our journey to have a safe landing. When I first considered taking a position in hospice, I was fixated on the word *hospice*, and the letters *h-o-p-e* from this word jumped off the page as if illuminated by a neon sign. HOPE. Most people think hospice is when there is nothing that can be done, when there no longer is hope. After some soul searching over several days, I realized that the message I was getting was "not hope to live forever" but rather "hope to end well" as I have since often voiced. I took the position which was the best thing I ever did. Ending well means being able to be with your family and loved ones, surrounded with love, free from spiritual pain, having the time to make any amends, to make necessary family and financial considerations, and to be at peace—to be able to say, "It is well with my soul."

Personal Legacy Building

Do you have your plans in place to end well? The loss of a loved one reinforces the point that you owe it to your family and friends to make known your wishes and plans for them to follow after you depart this world. If we have plans in place to end well, what do we do in the meantime, that is what do we do with our dash? We don't want to waste the learning experience that grief offers. Find ways to make some good come out of this experience. One man initially told me after losing his wife that "nothing good will ever come out of this." He has since demonstrated considerable personal growth. His loss was not in vain. Have faith in your resilience.

Journal Thoughts _____

_____

_____

_____

_____

_____

_____

_____

_____

_____

_____

Strategies for Creating Your Own Legacy

Who tells your story?

—Lin-Manuel Miranda, "Who Lives, Who Dies, Who Tells Your Story," from *Hamilton*

I can make a difference; I am making a difference. Yes, you need to humbly assert that you can make a difference, not only in the direction of your life, but also how it impacts others. Yes, you can, and you are making a difference.

ROAD SCHOLAR ASSIGNMENT: My Purpose and Meaning

Creating a Personal Mission Statement

Your personal mission statement is one or two sentences designed to help clarify your purpose in life. Take a moment to consider and write it now. You can revisit this later to revise.

My Personal Mission Statement

Creating Your Life Purpose Statement

To create your legacy and have a guide to your future, take a few minutes and contemplate your life purpose. Please remember, just as your world has been changed by your loss, so you too have been changed. Write it now, you can revisit this later to revise.

My Life Purpose Statement

- **The right (or "write") stuff**

   Write on! Right now! If you have been able to write your personal mission statement and your life purpose assignments listed above, then you are a writer. Keep writing. Those I work with tell me that writing a journal or taking a creative writing class has been instrumental in their healing and renewal. Tell your story, start by writing short vignettes in your journal. Write one-page entries on anything that comes to mind, from what you are feeling and thinking today, to a trivial moment or a momentous event from the past.

- **Just say "know" to nostalgia**

  Take a trip down memory lane, to some of the early years with your loved one, or perhaps even back to your childhood and teenage years. A remembrance trip may do you good, a remembrance and *gratitude* outing. Visit nostalgic places, such as schools, churches, diners, a childhood home, campsites. Eat s'mores, hot dogs, and all that, yes, indeed.

Truths from the Road: Continuing a Legacy

"We lost our forty-year-old son and we are honoring him by continuing to carry on his work of helping the homeless. This is our way of keeping his spirit alive."

"I've picked up where my wife left off," one man said continuing his wife's legacy of supporting a nonprofit agency.

- **Give back, get in the game, volunteer**

  To help others gives great meaning and purpose. We are at our best when helping others without pursuit of financial gain. Sometimes utilizing personal experiences from our tough times can help us heal and flourish. One woman told me that because of her husband's death with Alzheimer's, she was encouraged to become an advocate for Alzheimer's research through grassroots lobbying. A high percentage of our volunteers in hospice had a positive hospice experience with a loved one and they want to give back through volunteering. You are uniquely qualified to help in important ways as a volunteer if and when the time is right for you.

- **Lead a support group**

  A number of bereaved who have attended hospice support groups and workshops have gone on to assist or lead groups of their own at churches or community centers. Many community bereavement groups are peer-to-peer led rather than professionally led. Naturally, this is not for everyone and is for later in your journey when you have gained perspective and are ready to give back. Your loss gives you direct experience. You are the expert of you, knowing how grief has shaped you, what has worked and what has not worked for you. Your heart has been uniquely transformed and sharing your empathy may be just the ticket for finding meaning and purpose.

- **You are a legacy heir: claim your inheritance**

  I am not talking about money. Yes, you may be the financial heir and there may be a monetary inheritance. Rather, I am talking about you being the heir of the remembrance legacy left behind by your loved one. You are the heir or heiress to the memories and special moments that you created with your loved one. You are heir to all that you can hold onto that makes you smile from your days and years together. Put a claim to this special inheritance, it was earned by you and your loved one. Most importantly, please remember IT IS ENOUGH. Yes, in life we seem to come hardwired to always want a little more. That is OK, because for you, your inheritance is enough.

- **Embracing significance**

  Significance is the new success. Personal significance, not personal success, seems to be the emphasis for many after a loss. Those who have experienced a great loss often seek a greater work-life balance. They come to understand that this balance is more important than success. For some bereaved, their thinking soon turns to legacy building. They desire to end their lives well, by leaving behind the examples of lives well lived. The legacy of significance is available to each of us, regardless of circumstance.

ROAD SCHOLAR ASSIGNMENT: What Will Be My Legacy?

As you focus on your "new life" after loss, pause to ask: What will *my* legacy be? Take a moment to focus on your own legacy. Review your thoughts and preferences and put them in writing, either now or in the near future.

- Do you need to write a letter to loved ones, to be shared now or later?

- Do you have a living will and advanced directives?

- Is there anything you can do now or in the near future to help with your own legacy building?

- I want anyone interested to know this about my loved one . . .

- I want anyone interested to know this about myself . . .

- What personal qualities do you want to be known for *now* and in the *future*?

- How do you want to be *remembered*, and what *legacy* do you want to leave behind?

Destination Road: Welcome Home

Homeward bound / I wish I was

—Paul Simon, "Homeward Bound"

Truckin', I'm a goin' home.

—The Grateful Dead, "Truckin'"

And grace will lead me home.

—John Newton, "Amazing Grace"

Where Thou art—that—is Home.

—Emily Dickinson

There's no place like home.

—L. Frank Baum, *The Wonderful Wizard of Oz*

Welcome Home, You Are Home

Population: You

You are home. Imagine yourself pulling into your metaphorical driveway, you have arrived home, your destination. Arriving at your destination, you know that you have been personally renewed and transformed. Home for you is both an ending and a beginning. Home is now your new starting point, your new beginning on the road of life. Home is not a physical place—home is within you, home is where you are, where you are now sitting or standing. Home is where you belong—*at home with yourself.* Welcome home!

You Are Your Destination

Your Destination Equation

Doing + Being + Time = Destination

Destination = Home

Home = You

YOU are your destination!

Destination State of Mind: My Return Home

- *I am at peace*—Thankfulness and Gratitude
- *I am alive*—Joy and Happiness
- *I am whole*—Meaning and Purpose
- *I am healed*—Healing and Renewal
- *I am home*—Acceptance and Transformation

Your Destination Self-Check: How Will I Know I Am Home?

Your composite picture of your "destination self" is coming into focus. The following are inward and outward signs that you have arrived HOME.

You will know you have arrived home when . . .

- you experience outbreaks of joy and these "joy bursts" are more frequent and last longer.
- you are able to express thankfulness and gratitude for the special person you lost who helped shape who you are today.
- you are able to laugh again with more laughter and fewer tears.
- you no longer think incessantly of your deceased loved one.
- you gain a sense of satisfaction for getting out of your comfort zone and being willing to pursue new opportunities.
- you have enlisted new opportunities to be with people, gaining new friendships and reviving old friendships.
- you find yourself able to love life and to view it as a gift.
- you discover that solitude is becoming more comfortable and loneliness less threatening.
- you learn acceptance for yourself, your loss, and the world in which you live.
- you feel at peace, comfortable and alive in your own skin.
- you get your steering wheel back.

Home Is Your Daily Destination

A painting is never finished—it simply stops in interesting places.
—Paul Gardner

You are *home* today, at peace with yourself. You need to know that arriving home is not a one-and-done destination. Your destination expires each day, and you will need to be intentional to stay on your Destination Road. Life after loss requires one to be refreshed and renewed daily. You will always need to be moving forward, growing as a person, and giving back. Living life in this manner will perpetuate your legacy and that of your loved one. This is where you will find your joy.

Home Is Our Destination: Homecoming and Homegoing

"I don't know if I am coming or going" is a well-known saying. *Home* is where we do both, coming and going.

- **Homecoming Is of This World**

  HOMECOMING. Like the tradition of welcoming back alumni to a school or institution, this is your opportunity to be welcomed home after loss.

- **Homegoing Is of the Next World**

  HOMEGOING. This, too, is your opportunity to know your ultimate waypoint on your life's Destination Road. "Homegoing" is the African American funeral tradition which celebrates the going home of the deceased to heaven. When your life's work and journey on Earth is finished, you too will have going home as your ultimate destination.

Heaven on Earth: Is It in Reach?

Earth's crammed with heaven, / And every common bush afire with God.
—Elizabeth Barrett Browning, "Aurora Leigh"

Waiting for the spark from heaven to fall.
—Matthew Arnold, "The Scholar-Gipsy"

Heaven is under our feet as well as over our heads.
—Henry David Thoreau,
"The Pond in Winter," *Walden*, (sign posted in a patient's garden)

Heaven on Earth is not a place, but a state of being. This is available to all of us, no matter our physical health, economic situation, or social standing. Working in hospice with end-of-life care, we often hear heartfelt stories of our patients having glimpses of heaven in their final days. As patients transition from this life to the next, we hear comforting stories of angels and deceased loved ones welcoming them home in visions.

Glimpses of heaven are not reserved for the end of life. While we are here, our aim should be to experience as much of heaven on Earth as humanly possible. To have joy in our lives certainly honors our creator and belief system. I am hopeful you will capture glimpses of heaven on Earth. Then you will know you have reached your earthly destination of healthy healing from your significant loss. *Is a glimpse of heaven on Earth coming soon to you?*

Heaven, Your Ultimate Destination?

Heaven is my home, but I am not homesick.
      —Unknown

Wouldn't it be loverly.
—Alan Jay Lerner and Frederick Loewe, from *My Fair Lady*

Heaven is the answer. In workshops I have led, when grievers are asked what is the ultimate destination for them, by far the most universal response is "heaven." Naturally, those who have faith in God or a higher power probably see life on Earth as their temporary destination. Your ultimate destination will likely be *heaven* or whatever name you ascribe to it. Take a moment to consider being heaven bound, that you will be home*going* to your heavenly home, or "heaven house" as aptly described by a nine-year-old granddaughter of one of our hospice patients. Speaking of heaven, one woman said, "I don't have to worry about my husband, he's home now." It is a wonderful gift if you have this faith. If we have faith in our homegoing to heaven, then shouldn't we also have faith and a great appreciation for the gift of life from our creator for our home*coming* here on Earth? Let's lift a toast to life!

Journal Thoughts _____

_____

_____

_____

_____

_____

_____

_____

Epilogue

When my soul was in the lost-and-found

—Carole King, "(You Make Me Feel Like) A Natural Woman"

I once was lost but now am found

—John Newton, "Amazing Grace"

This is a book of lost and found. I am so hopeful that you have been able to *find* your *lost* self, after the loss of your loved one. People often say grief never ends. People ask if it is possible to move beyond grief? One thing I know is that memories never end. I also know for certain that LOVE NEVER ENDS. I have also been told, "one day I woke up, and the page seemed to turn. I decided to move forward with my life!" Here we are, perfectly imperfect, and perfectly human. You have reached the pinnacle, the mountaintop, rarefied air. A glimpse of heaven on Earth. And life goes on, what a wonderful world.

THE END (and Beginning)

And I think to myself what a wonderful world.

—sung by Louis Armstrong

Congratulations for running the race and staying the course. I admire your courageous spirit. Enjoy an ice-cream cone or favorite treat, you deserve it. You have traveled a long distance. *One for the road!* Moving forward, please keep this book handy for future reference when you need a tune-up.

Thank you for allowing me to be your guide on your *Hard and Beautiful Road.* The best is yet to be! The husband of one of my patients, a deceased Illinois farmer, was well-known for his cheery "keep your chin up" goodbyes to everyone he met, so thank you for being YOU and in his words . . . **Keep your tailgate up.**

Acknowledgments

My heartfelt thanks to my beautiful and loving wife, Llinos, and to my wonderful family for putting up with me during the writing process. They have been so understanding and totally supportive, allowing me the time to work on this project. Thank you, Llinos, for carefully reading and collaborating with me on all aspects of this book, I truly appreciate it. I would like to thank my son, Matt, for contributing such great illustrations. It was a joy to work together.

I am grateful for my mentor and friend, author and renowned grief expert Dr. Harold Ivan Smith for his careful reading and important and thoughtful suggestions for improvements to this book.

I would like to thank the following people who have recently grieved the loss of a loved one, for reading the manuscript and offering valuable suggestions from the perspective of the bereaved: Tom Smitko, John Newman, and Mary Joan Johnston. Your insights and perspective made this book better and will be of great value to others who have suffered loss.

Special thanks to Mary Kay Speaks for her very capable and excellent editing of the manuscript and helping shepherd it through to its completion. Thank you, Mary Kay, for your attention to detail and for your invaluable recommendations. Many thanks to Jack Martin for his skilled graphic layout and excellent cover design.

I would like to thank my good friend Dr. Gary Ripple who encouraged me to work in hospice and has been an encourager for this project from the beginning. I would also like to thank Amy Kitsembel, my fellow counterpart in bereavement from Wisconsin, for her encouragement and support for this book.

I also am indebted to my colleagues at Saint Luke's Home Care & Hospice for the opportunity to learn from and to be wowed by their selfless dedication to our patients and families.

This book is inspired by those who are grieving or have grieved that I work with daily. It has truly been an honor and privilege to walk by your side, and this book would not have been possible without you. Thank you!

To the Reader:
A Note of Thanks
and a Request

I so appreciate that you have traveled this road with me. If you have any suggestions to improve this book for future editions, I would love to hear from you. If this book resonated with you, I ask you to take a few moments to write a review, and recommend the book to anyone who you think would benefit from reading it. The secret of healing after loss is to help others, and any feedback would be helpful to future grievers.

For additional information or to schedule a speaking engagement, workshop, or personal counseling session, please visit *www.griefroadmap.com*.

About the Author

Bruce Leisy is a hospice grief and bereavement counselor for Saint Luke's Homecare & Hospice, an agency of Saint Luke's Health System in Kansas City, Missouri. Bruce is an ADEC certified grief counselor specializing in loss, grief, and bereavement. His wife, Llinos, a native of Britain, works as a Volunteer and Community Events Coordinator at Saint Luke's Hospice House. They have lived in Oxford, New Hampshire, Boston, Athens, Wichita, London, and Princeton, where they have enjoyed careers in independent school education and small business ownership. Bruce is the author of the book, *A History of the Leisy Brewing Companies*. Bruce holds degrees from Bethel College and University of New Hampshire and completed his studies at Oxford University. They have two adult children and two grandchildren and live in Kansas City, Missouri.

Journal Thoughts _____

Made in the USA
Monee, IL
02 March 2020